Walking in
His Garden

Spending Quality Time with God

DISCOVERY HOUSE

PUBLISHERS®

Contents

PREFACE

We all know that a steady diet of prayer and Bible reading is the secret to improving our relationship with the Lord, but sometimes we struggle with implementation.

That's why we have collected four Discovery Series booklets and compiled them in one book. In this book we have provided you with some practical help for establishing a meaningful time with God, a series of profound and practical guidelines for effective prayer, and a refresher course in how to get the most out of your Bible reading.

It is our hope that as you improve your prayer life and enhance your Bible reading, you'll find new joy in *Walking In His Garden* as you "grow in the grace and knowledge of our Lord and Savior Jesus Christ" (2 Peter 3:18).

ONE

Keeping Our Appointments With God

What if we could find a place to meet quietly with someone who loves us—someone who accepts us just as we are, while seeing in us far more than we see in ourselves? What if this person could relieve our stress, our guilt, our insecurity, and our boredom?

If such a place and such a person existed, we can be sure that our enemy would try to talk us out of going there. Yet, as RBC writer Dennis Fisher shows us in the following pages, the place and the Person are waiting for us. What remains is for us to find practical ways of wearing a path to Him.

May the God of all peace fill you with joy as together we learn to walk with Him in the quiet and rush of our days.

MARTIN R. DE HAAN II

Stressed By Life's Demands

A middle-age executive nervously organizes his weekly calendar, having heard that mid-management downsizing will begin next month.

A young mother of twin toddlers struggles to get some time to herself, but the children keep waking each other up from their afternoon nap.

A recent high-school graduate with a newly shaved head struggles for privacy in his bunk at Marine Corps basic training.

The examples mentioned above are busy people who want to walk with God throughout the day. Yet all three have one thing in common. Each is in an environment that makes it difficult to spend quality time with God in prayer and Bible reading. It's precisely when we are stressed by life's demands that a time of spiritual refocus becomes so important.

Many of us live with a sense of guilt because we are neglecting our personal devotional time with God. During the hectic demands of the day, it's easy to let the care of our inner life fall by the wayside.

But if we measure our spirituality by counting the times we have met with God during the week, we have missed the point. Devotions are a matter of our heart more than a discipline of our daytimer.

Right after the creation of the first man and woman, God is seen "walking in the garden in the cool of the day" (Gen. 3:8). The Sovereign of the universe did not hide behind closed doors and ask angelic executive assistants to keep His creatures out. Instead, He took the initiative to seek out Adam and Eve for spiritual companionship.

A healthy and consistent devotional time is one important way we can respond to

> Devotions are a matter of our heart more than a discipline of our daytimer.

God's desire to walk with us. Couples who are in love do not need to be coerced into spending time together. Each has a deep longing to experience life in relationship with the other person. When life's interruptions keep them apart, each one seeks opportunities to reconnect.

That is what the quiet time is all about. We want to spend time with God to experience His presence, comfort, and guidance. And in a mysterious way, as we spend time with God "beholding as in a mirror the glory of the Lord, [we] are being transformed into the same image" (2 Cor. 3:18). We find that spending time with God actually changes the kind of people we are.

This chapter is a short, practical guide to how to "reconnect with God." It is designed to help you seek the One who created you for a relationship with Him and to encourage you to draw upon His strength to live a growing spiritual life. In short, it is a guide to "keep our appointments with God" because of what He has done for us.

A Relational Approach To Spending Time With God

S uccessful marriages are as diverse as the variety of snowflakes. Athletes marry artistic types, and social butterflies marry the shy and retiring. The differences can be a source of conflict. Yet with a growing understanding of one's self and one's spouse, each can learn to adapt to the other's idiosyncrasies for the long haul.

Our walk with God is much like a spiritual marriage. Jesus Christ, the Bridegroom, has sought us out for eternal relationship. Because each of us has a different temperament, uses a different thought process, and is at a different level of spiritual maturity, each possesses a unique relationship with Christ. Jesus, our Good Shepherd, is well aware of our individuality and wants to give us just what we need to grow in our walk with Him. As we study the Bible, we learn more and more about His amazing personal qualities and compassion for us. And in response to His overtures of love, we will want to find time to spend with Him.

The same fellowship-seeking God who walked in the cool of the day with Adam and Eve is reaching out to each of us today. But when should we try to connect with Him?

Many people emphasize the importance of starting the day with devotions. I once heard someone say that the guiding code for his own devotional life was "No Bible, no breakfast." But depending on your metabolism and current lifestyle, you may be more mentally alert at midday, or even late at night. Everyone is different.

The Bible encourages meeting with God during any of these times. David wrote, "O God, You are my God; early will I seek You" (Ps. 63:1). Nehemiah, the great reformer, "read [the Law] . . . from morning to midday" (Neh. 8:3). David mentioned his anticipation to meditate on God's Word during the "night watches" (Ps. 119:148). And Psalm 1 refers to the blessed man whose "delight is in the law of the Lord, and in His law he meditates day and night" (v. 2).

The Bible provides wonderful freedom about when to meet with God. The central issue is not what your metabolism is like but rather what time of day will work best for you and your schedule. In my current situation, I find morning to be a good time. Often I will read a passage in the morning, reflect on it during the day, and review it again in the evening. It helps to have the same biblical thought throughout the day.

What matters most is to establish a regular time when God can speak to you through His Word and you can respond to Him in prayer. Once you have chosen a time, it's important to be disciplined in keeping your appointments with God. But how?

BUILDING A RELATIONSHIP

"Everyone who competes for the prize is temperate in all things" (1 Cor. 9:25).

Two people who love each other are intentional about spending meaningful time together. To do this, both discipline and love must work together. Taking time requires deliberate planning.

A similar focus is necessary to cultivate meaningful time with God. Often we begin the day fully intent on having devotions at a set time. But as the day goes on, we are bombarded by one urgent item after another. Soon devotions are postponed until tomorrow.

But when a quiet time is the priority, centering ourselves in God puts things in perspective. And this relational connection requires discipline.

In 1 Corinthians 9, the apostle Paul used the imagery of athletic games to illustrate the need for spiritual discipline. The term used for "temperate" really means "the power of self-control; to practice abstinence."

When athletes say "yes" to the Olympics, they say "no" to other distractions. Rigorous control of diet and exercise is the only way to win in their chosen competitive sport.

Similarly, by setting up a daily devotional discipline and making it the priority, a host of other positive habits can follow.

Here are some ways to set up a quiet time before you actually begin:

Reserve A Daily Time To Reconnect

Whether we need a highly disciplined schedule or prefer a more relaxed one, we all need a plan. If you are using a daily planner, computer software, or some other calendar, you might want to set aside a time when you will meet with God daily.

Determine How Much Time To Spend

When I was taking classical guitar lessons, the instructor told me, "It's better to practice 15 minutes a day every day, and then to practice for several hours on only a few days." He was right, especially when it comes to establishing new habits. But new habits are sometimes hard to form.

It's not by accident that the author of Hebrews wrote that we are not to forsake "the assembling of ourselves together, as is the manner of some" (Heb. 10:25). He understood that church attendance, like any other activity, is a habit that needs to be cultivated.

This principle clearly applies to our devotional time. It's better to block out 15 minutes and seek to remain faithful to honoring that time than it is to let our daily discipline be eaten away by daily distractions. After praying about how much time to spend, enter that time block into your calendar.

Find A Quiet Place

We all concentrate or are distracted in different ways. C. S. Lewis brings up a surprising suggestion in his book *Letters To Malcolm*. His admonition on the "quiet time" is to make sure we have "just the right amount of distraction" to help us concentrate. Lewis tells the story of a man who would have his devotional time in a railway compartment because complete silence left him open to inner distractions. Ironically, his focus was enhanced when it was challenged just slightly.

> Daily devotions are about progress more than perfection.

The point is that we're not always going to find a place that is as quiet as an undiscovered cave. Invariably, minor distractions are likely to occur. But we need to look for a place where we believe it is sufficiently quiet to help us concentrate.

Now jot down in your calendar the place for re-connecting with the Lord.

Set Up Realistic Expectations

I knew a student a number of years ago who was an excellent writer. The problem was that he always turned in his papers late. Why?

"If I can't do it right, I won't do it!" was his response. His commitment to perfectionism led him down a path of inconsistency. This is a common problem in maintaining a quiet time. It is a "throwing the baby out with the bath water" mentality. It is the "all or nothing" approach to a devotional life.

But in a realistic sense, daily devotions are about progress more than perfection. It's better for us to have a shorter and even less meaningful devotional time on a given day than it is to skip it in the name of high standards. When we wait for the perfect circumstances to have "quality time" with the Lord, they rarely occur. Manageable bite-size devotional times can lead to greater consistency.

But what happens when the time and place are reserved and you actually show up for your quiet time, but you're not in the mood to have one?

EXCHANGING HUMAN STRENGTH FOR DIVINE STRENGTH

"Those who wait on the Lord shall renew [exchange] their strength" (Isa. 40:31).

Isaiah believed that waiting on the Lord was anything but a passive process. This idea of "staying power" required a radical exchange of human for divine strength. The Hebrew word for *renew* means "to substitute, to exchange, to show newness, to sprout." The Christian is not supposed to stir up his or her willpower but instead to exchange human energy for divine energy.

When I was a sophomore in college, I had a discipline problem when it came to studying. I found all kinds of other activities with my friends that competed with getting assignments in on time and being fully prepared for exams.

One night after class, I discussed my problem with one of my professors. After talking to him, I felt compelled to single out my devotional time as the top priority of the day. It would be the one project I planned on getting done first thing every morning.

The next day as I began my new commitment to prioritize my quiet time, I found a sudden sagging in my resolve. I just didn't feel like doing it. I was not in the mood.

Claiming Isaiah 40:31, I decided to become transparent with the Lord and "exchange my strength" for His. I told Him my heart was cold and that I felt little motivation to spend time with Him. I confessed my apathy as sin, and then I thanked Him for His forgiveness (1 Jn. 1:9).

> The Christian is not supposed to stir up his or her willpower, but instead to exchange human energy for divine energy.

Then I chose to surrender my mood to God and asked Him to change it. I began to depend on Him to replace my stagnation with His vitality. I read through the biblical passage again that I was scheduled to read. I recommitted myself to pray for transformation.

After about 20 minutes of this, I began to pray over other projects that needed my attention later in the day. I told God about assignments I didn't want to do and asked Him for the strength necessary to deal with them.

By the time my feet hit the asphalt on my way to class, I began to feel an energy, a focus, and most important, a discipline that I had previously lacked.

My grades went up that semester. I had found a way of exchanging my strength for that of the living God.

CULTIVATING TWO-WAY COMMUNICATION

Have you ever written a letter to someone in which you really opened your heart? You probably felt vulnerable as you waited for a response. How would you feel if the written response to your letter ignored everything you had said but talked only about issues that concerned the other person?

This could be the view of heaven as many a quiet time goes on day in and day out. The Bible is a love letter from our heavenly Father. Yet too often our prayers do not reflect the actual portion of Scripture we have read. Instead, the content of the love letter is ignored as our many pressing needs are petitioned upward.

What needs to happen, however, is spiritual two-way communication.

God Speaks To Us Through His Word

First Samuel 3:21 says that "the Lord revealed Himself to Samuel . . . by the word of the Lord." The Hebrew word for *reveal* means "to show or uncover." The Creator discloses His thoughts, character, and will through His Word. In biblical history, God either spoke directly or inspired His meanings into the sacred text. Today, He illuminates the Bible so we can have our understanding enlightened by the Holy Spirit as we read it.

In approaching a portion of Scripture, there is a time-honored process that can help make examining the Word of God fruitful.

First, we need to ask, "**What does the passage say?**" We answer this by looking at the actual words of the text as they are used in context. Allow the Bible passage to speak for itself in its original historical and cultural setting. For example, let the Bible character wear his robe and sandals instead of expecting him to wear a business suit.

The second step is to ask, "**What does it mean?**" Within the Bible passage is an eternal spiritual truth that is meaningful in all ages. Often the main idea is not time-bound to an era hundreds of years ago but can be seen in our own time's contemporary clothing.

Finally, we need to ask, "**How does it apply?**" The indwelling Holy Spirit will change our thoughts, speech, and behavior when we allow Him to use the spiritual principles we find in God's Word. A key question to ask is, "In what measurable ways should my life change as a result of studying this passage?"

Now let's look at our conversational response to God.

We Respond To God In Prayer

Daniel 6:10 says that Daniel "prayed and gave thanks before his God, as was his custom since early days." A group of the king's advisors knew about Daniel's prayer habit and plotted to use it against him. They were angry and jealous that the king was considering giving Daniel political power. So they influenced the king to pass an edict that would put to death anyone who prayed to any god or man other than the king himself. Yet, despite the danger, Daniel kept his appointment with God at an open window as he had always done.

During this established time of prayer, Daniel undoubtedly petitioned God about his own personal needs and interceded on behalf of the needs of others.

As Daniel was making his requests known to God, a spirit of thanksgiving permeated his prayer-time. The whole idea of giving thanks carries with it the

> "[Daniel] prayed and gave thanks before his God, as was his custom."
> —DANIEL 6:10 (NIV)

idea of gratefully responding to God for gifts already given. It is part of the dialogue that expresses appreciation. Immersion in the Word has a way of serving as a springboard of praise to God for who He is and what He has done for us.

TAKING TIME TO DIGEST YOUR MEAL

"Your words were found, and I ate them, and Your word was to me the joy and rejoicing of my heart; for I am called by Your name, O Lord God of hosts" (Jer. 15:16).

A delicious meal is not very appealing if you experience indigestion afterward. Slowing the intake of the Word through careful reflection is also essential.

When encountering the pages of the Bible, it is so easy to skim over a given passage without seeing its significance. But the prophet Jeremiah, with his deep love for the Word of God, made it his first priority. The Hebrew word translated "were found" means both "to acquire and secure" and "to encounter and meet." When looking at a passage, we should slow down and acquaint ourselves with the text until it becomes secured in our soul.

The passage then refers to one of the most enjoyable aspects of the culinary experience—actually eating the food. The word *eat* can mean "devouring, consuming food" as well as "burning fuel like a fire." When we begin to "chew" on a passage we begin to taste the wonderful spiritual flavors it contains.

Have you ever been hungry and found yourself sitting down to a wide range of entrees with distinctive flavors? As your stomach begins to fill with protein, fat, and carbohydrates, you actually begin to feel a lifting of your mood emotionally. Jeremiah felt a rush of "joy and rejoicing" as he ingested God's Word into his heart. The word the prophet used for "heart" means "the inner man, thinking, reflection at the seat of appetites." The Word of God nourishes our thoughts and emotions, and brings joy.

The foundation for delighting in feeding on God's Word can be seen in the concluding section of this small but meaningful verse: "I am called by

Your name, O Lord God of hosts." To Jeremiah, meaningful time in God's Word is always tied to our relationship with Him. In our devotional time, we become aware once again that we are called by the eternally existing Lord of heaven and earth. And this realization transforms our spiritual dryness into a dynamic encounter with the One who created us for fellowship with Him.

WRITING IT DOWN

Without getting buried in paperwork, there are some advantages to writing down your personal time with the Lord.

Our thoughts and feelings are a constant revolving door of varied life experiences. If we have a written record of what is covered in our quiet time, various trends in our walk of faith will be revealed.

> When looking at a passage, we should slow down and acquaint ourselves with the text until it becomes secured in our soul.

In addition to this, we will see progress that has been made in different areas of our lives that would go unnoticed if it were not written down.

The guide given on the next page could be copied down in a notebook and kept as a concise record of your daily quiet time.

DEVOTIONAL GUIDE

Date:_____

Passage Read Today: _____

Version:_____

Highlight (chapter & verse): _____

_____

Insights: _____

_____

_____

Application:_____

_____

_____

Prayer time:_____

_____

_____

_____

VARYING YOUR METHODS

R ecently I was at a local Christian bookstore doing some browsing. I asked the woman behind the counter about books to help with daily devotions. She took me over to a whole section of different helps for a personal quiet time.

There was a popular day-by-day devotional. Not far from it was *My Utmost For His Highest* by Oswald Chambers, a devotional classic adapted for a daily quiet time. Farther down the aisle was another selection of readings for going through the Bible in one year.

In most of these books, a relevant inspirational excerpt or story draws a lesson from a suggested Bible reading. One reason for the popularity of this kind of devotional guide is that it has a short, memorable lesson that is both inspiring and applicable to daily life.

One caution in using this kind of guide, however, is the temptation to just read the story and skip the Bible reading for the day. Once this becomes a habit, the believer can find his life built on inspirational thoughts instead of the Word of God—a spiritual life that is built on very shaky ground.

If you use one of these devotional guides, be sure to read the Bible passage along with the stories that illustrate the biblical truth. If we build our lives on anecdotes and excerpts rather than on the Word of God, we can develop an improper view of the Christian life, and we may be setting ourselves up for a fall. God has promised to bless His Word—not our illustrations about it (2 Tim. 3:15-16).

In addition to the wonderful resources for daily devotions that you can find in any Christian bookstore, there are Web sites where additional help can be found (see www.crosswalk.com).

There is such a variety of different methods for effective devotional times and Bible study that there's bound to be a suitable approach for you.

In our drive to make our method work, it's important to remind ourselves about our motivation. Spending time with God to experience His presence, comfort, and guidance should be our goal—not to be more "spiritual" or to alleviate guilt for our own shortcomings.

Consider the example of the Lord Jesus Christ. He was perfect and never sinned, yet He looked for undistracted time with His Father. Why? Because Jesus functioned on earth as every human being was intended to function—in total dependence on the Father. Let's take a look at how He sought out time to commune with His heavenly Father.

Jesus' Priority Of Prayer

In Mark 1:35-39 we see the priority that Jesus put on prayer. After an exhausting time of healing sick and demon-possessed people late into the night, Jesus woke early in the morning, went to a solitary place, and prayed. I believe that Jesus used this time for regaining His spiritual center. Peter interrupted Jesus' devotional time to express the further demands of the needy crowd. Rather than responding to the immediate need, the Lord reaffirmed a commitment to greater outreach in other cities.

A closer look at the text will show the inner workings of our Lord's own devotional life.

SEEKING ISOLATION AND COMMUNION

"Now in the morning, having risen a long while before daylight, He went out and departed to a solitary place; and there He prayed" (Mk. 1:35).

Have you ever thought about why Jesus Christ even needed a quiet time? We are all aware of our own weaknesses and sins. The need for cleansing and renewal is often the felt need of the committed believer. But the Bible teaches the sinlessness of our Lord—He "who knew no sin" (2 Cor. 5:21). So why did Jesus go out to a solitary place while the disciples slept in?

During His ministry on earth, the Lord Jesus chose to limit the exercise of His divine attributes. He was fully God, but He chose to depend on the Father and the indwelling Spirit working through Him. He did this to show us how we are to depend on God. That dependence can be seen in the way Jesus sought time alone with His Father. The term translated "solitary place" means "a desert, wasteland, uninhabited region." After such dynamic emotional interactions as healing many crippled and sick from the night before, Christ needed solitude to make communion with the Father most effective.

> The walk of faith requires coming repeatedly to God for His unique guidance.

The walk of faith requires coming repeatedly to God for His unique guidance. The result of Jesus' time alone with God redirected His vision from local needs to greater outreach.

LISTENING TO GOD'S DIRECTION AMID DISTRACTION

"Simon and those who were with Him searched for Him. When they found Him, they said to Him, 'Everyone is looking for You.' But He said to them, 'Let us go into the next towns, that I may preach there also, because for this purpose I have come forth'" (Mk. 1:36-38).

The word found in verse 37 is better translated "hunted down." Can you imagine a more annoying scenario? Peter thought he knew best how Christ should spend His day. And he was even willing to interrupt the Lord's prayer-time to offer his advice. The need Simon Peter expressed was clearly an urgent one: "Everyone is looking for You."

No one active in ministry (either fulltime or as a volunteer) has escaped the pressure of certain ministry "interest groups." Their needs are often valid, and they sometimes have representatives who plead for immediate attention. Yet look at what Jesus did. He was not worried about being perceived as someone who wasn't responsive to immediate needs. Having only a limited amount of time and energy, He had received direction from His Father to go elsewhere.

You would think Jesus' quiet time would have made Him more sensitive to the people right there with Him. But to meet only the needs directly in front of us is to ignore God's ever-expanding concern for those who are lost. Time alone with His Father brought Jesus back to the purpose for which He came into the world: "to seek and to save that which was lost" (Lk. 19:10).

CARRYING OUT APPLICATION
"He was preaching in their synagogues throughout all Galilee, and casting out demons" (Mk. 1:39).

It's easy to skip over the significance of the last verse of this section. It's not just a review of the previous verse. Verse 39 is the payoff to the whole passage.

Jesus actually did what He said He was going to do. He went to the synagogues and preached.

The word *preaching* would be used over and over again within the pages of the New Testament as the apostles duplicated the Lord's pattern for spreading the good news in expanding circles of outreach. Jesus' target area for ministry was expanded to include "all Galilee." Later, as His disciples followed in His steps, it would extend "to the end of the earth" (Acts 1:8).

It's important to apply what comes out of our prayer-time. Meaningful fellowship with Christ comes when we follow His example (1 Pet. 2:21) and apply His Word in the power of the Spirit.

Jesus said, "He who has My commandments and keeps them, it is he who loves Me. And he who loves Me will be loved by My Father, and I will love him and manifest Myself to him" (Jn. 14:21). If we see our quiet time only as a spiritual oasis once a day, we may fall into the trap of compartmentalizing our spiritual life. From the Garden of Eden until now, God has desired to walk with His people in life's journey (Gen. 3:8). So it's essential that we take what we learn in our quiet time with us throughout the entire day.

Carrying The Divine Dialogue Into The Day

Our Lord's encounter in Luke 24:13-32 with the two men walking on the Emmaus Road is filled with insights about how to keep the divine dialogue with God going throughout the day.

ENCOUNTERING JESUS IN REAL-LIFE PROBLEMS

Have you ever poured a lot of spiritual attention into your quiet time and then left it behind to face the problems of the day in your own strength? This is called compartmentalization or confining your spiritual life to an exclusive part of the day. But Jesus never intended for us to go it alone. He is eager to help us solve life's problems. Let's take a look at how He did this on the road to Emmaus.

> *Now behold, two of them were traveling that same day to a village called Emmaus, which was seven miles from Jerusalem. And they talked together of all these things which had happened. So it was, while they conversed and reasoned, that Jesus Himself drew near and went with them. But their eyes were restrained, so that they did not know Him (Lk. 24:13-16).*

Little is known about the two who walked the

well-worn path from Jerusalem to the village of Emmaus. But the Bible indicates that they were troubled. They had an internal conflict, an emotional struggle that was based on a disappointing experience. And this problem was being discussed by these two friends. Human beings are problem solvers by nature, and they usually don't do it alone.

It was in this context of human need that Jesus approached the two men as they walked. "Jesus Himself drew near and went with them" (v.15). What wonderful words! The risen Christ really does want to invade our human circumstances and carry on a dialogue with us. Life is a journey and Christ wants to be our companion on it, not just someone we talked to at the last rest stop.

TRYING TO MAKE SENSE OF GOD'S WAYS

One of the great challenges of the Christian life is trying to make sense of the apparent contradictions and setbacks we all face. Much of our perplexity comes from having only part of the whole picture, which distorts our perspective. The two men on the road to Emmaus illustrate this inadequacy and how the Lord Jesus helped them correct it.

[Jesus] said to them, "What kind of conversation is this that you have with one another as you walk and are sad?" Then the one whose name was Cleopas answered and said to Him, "Are you the only stranger in

Jerusalem, and have You not known the things which happened there in these days?" And He said to them, "What things?" So they said to Him, "The things concerning Jesus of Nazareth, who was a Prophet mighty in deed and word before God and all the people, and how the chief priests and our rulers delivered Him to be condemned to death, and crucified Him. But we were hoping that it was He who was going to redeem Israel. Indeed, besides all this, today is the third day since these things happened. Yes, and certain women of our company, who arrived at the tomb early, astonished us. When they did not find His body, they came saying that they had also seen a vision of angels who said He was alive. And certain of those who were with us went to the tomb and found it just as the women had said; but Him they did not see" (Lk. 24:17-24).

> One of the great challenges of the Christian life is trying to make sense of the apparent contradictions and setbacks we all face.

In response to Christ's question, the two went into detail about what was troubling them. Their summary is a concise review of the hope that Jesus of Nazareth was the Messiah who would redeem the nation Israel. Instead, He had been put to death in the most cruel form of execution—crucifixion. And to make their thoughts even more agitated, there had been reports of His tomb being empty and the appearance of angelic messengers.

The two who walked next to the Lord were troubled by soaring hopes followed by shattered dreams. Their experience is similar to what many of us have experienced. To be human is to look at life's events through a keyhole. Each of us is finite and can take in only part of the picture of any circumstance.

So often what we believe the Bible teaches doesn't make sense in our limited perspective of an apparent tragedy. Whether it's our expectations of how God should answer a prayer or how we view life's apparent misfortunes, we are limited in our understanding.

But Jesus wants us to tell Him our concerns. He has a listening ear and is concerned about all the details of our lives. Our unique relationship with Christ allows us to communicate with Him through prayer in any of life's experiences.

LETTING JESUS EXPLAIN HIMSELF

It must have been devastating for Jesus' followers to have their hopes and dreams crushed right in front of their eyes. But when Christ was allowed to illuminate their understanding of the Word of God in their experience, they began to get a fresh outlook on their circumstances.

Then He said to them, "O foolish ones, and slow of heart to believe in all that the prophets have spoken! Ought not the Christ to have suffered these things and to enter into His glory?" And beginning at Moses and all the Prophets, He expounded to them in all the Scriptures the things concerning Himself (Lk. 24:25-27).

Our Lord's response sounds abrupt. Yet in reality, this situation is a case study in education. Look at the wording. "Foolish ones" is a compound word that literally means "without knowledge." The disciples on the Emmaus Road were handicapped by having only part of the information.

"Slow of heart to believe" is a rebuke of their slowness in trusting God for what He had promised.

Jesus then provided the only remedy for spiritual ignorance—more information. The Teacher focused their attention on key passages of the Old Testament that explained that the Messiah must suffer before being glorified.

The lesson for us today is that though we may sometimes struggle with disappointment, we often lack all the information to make sense of it at the time. The Lord may eventually provide the people or the necessary information to bring closure to our problem. In some cases, we won't get the answer until we meet Christ face-to-face in eternity. But because life on earth is a spiritual bootcamp of sorts, it's essential to be teachable and in regular contact with our Teacher. Then our faith and knowledge can grow.

LEARNING TO KEEP THE CONVERSATION GOING

Meaningful connection with the risen Christ makes us want to linger in His presence. When the two travelers reached their final destination, they felt a strong need to stay in close proximity to the Savior.

> *Then they drew near to the village where they were going, and He indicated that He would have gone farther. But they constrained Him, saying, "Abide with us, for it is toward evening, and the day is far spent." And He went in to stay with them (Lk. 24:28-29).*

The disciples had several miles to hear what this "mysterious stranger" had to say, and they wanted to hear more. "Abide with us," was their response. They wanted to show hospitality to the One who had given such insight into messianic prophecy.

We all have times when our circumstances either nurture or hinder our spiritual development. We need to be sensitive to those times when we begin to lose contact with the Lord. Then we need to find ways of adapting to those circumstances so that we can reestablish our closeness to Him.

RESPONDING TO GLIMPSES OF DIVINE ACTIVITY

The stranger who had walked with the two on their journey joined them for their evening meal. And because of who their guest was, this meal would be accented with the supernatural. To include the Lord in our daily routine often results in seeing His divine activity at work.

Now it came to pass, as He sat at the table with them, that He took bread, blessed and broke it, and gave it to them. Then their eyes were opened and they knew Him; and He vanished from their sight. And they said to one another, "Did not our heart burn within us while He talked with us on the road, and while He opened the Scriptures to us?" (vv. 30-32).

At dinner that night, after Jesus broke the bread and blessed it, the disciples' eyes were opened and they recognized Him. Earlier, their eyes "were restrained, so that they did not know Him" (v. 16). But now their eyes were opened.

It's interesting that the word for "opened" has the same root as the word for "foolish and ignorant." An addition to this root word gives the word *opened* in verse 31 the meaning "to penetrate the mind." And once their minds understood who Jesus was, they recognized Him from previous encounters.

Surprisingly, the supernatural disappearance of our Lord didn't inspire any recorded comment between the two. Instead, they reflected on what it was like to be on the road talking with Jesus about the Scriptures.

> Recognizing Christ in the Scriptures and in our life experiences should occur throughout the day.

Their hearts were aflame with supernatural insight as Jesus Himself explained the Old Testament along the way. The same Greek word used for opening their eyes to recognize Him (v.31) is used to explain how He "opened the Scriptures" to them (v.32). He penetrated their minds with understanding.

Recognizing Christ in the Scriptures and in our life experiences should occur throughout the day rather than being limited to a once-a-day event.

So what can we learn from this incident with the resurrected Lord about extending our quiet time into the day?

- Learn how to pray while "on the go."
- Let God into your daily problem-solving activities.
- Acknowledge to others your need of divine help.
- Expect God to act outside your own limited perspective.
- Keep reflecting on a biblical theme for the day.
- Be encouraged by the fact that Jesus has promised to stay with us in all of life's circumstances.

Springboard
To Praise

How do we know if we're making progress in our personal time with the Lord? One major characteristic will be an increase in appreciation for who and what God is. Our personal quiet time should cause us to praise Him.

The apostle Paul taught about and practiced the dynamic relationship between God's Word and a lifestyle of praise:

> *Let the Word of Christ dwell in you richly in all wisdom, teaching and admonishing one another in psalms and hymns and spiritual songs, singing with grace in your hearts to the Lord (Colossians 3:16).*

When we personalize and internalize the Word of Christ, we make a place in our heart where He can feel at home. As this becomes a daily reality, we are moved to teach and admonish and learn from others about the wonders of God's character and His works. This results in instruction and encouragement, stimulating other people to praise God as well.

A healthy and meaningful devotional time spills over into three types of praise. "Psalms" are "Scripture songs" that have been lifted out of the pages of the Bible and set to music. "Hymns" are those melodies and lyrics that express an individual's personal relationship with God. And "spiritual songs" refer to a variety of worship lyrics and styles of music. What they all have in common is genuine spiritual content that reflects upon God's greatness.

The final portion of verse 16 underscores one of the unique distinctives of the Christian life—the realization of God's grace. Our quiet time should be forever linked to gratitude for the grace of God. It is a recognition that God has saved us from the penalty of sin and now provides the power to walk in obedience to Him.

An amazing characteristic of being in love is wanting to please the one you love. Our ongoing daily time with the Lord will help to increase our love for Him and enable us to please Him in all that we do.

When God spent personal time with the newly created Adam, walking with him in the Garden, it must have been a wonderful time of love, joy, and peace. Today, we too can have a moment-by-moment revitalizing exchange with God.

Have You Started Your Journey With Christ?

Our purpose in these pages has been to encourage a thoughtful, daily, heart-to-heart relationship with God. We've written primarily to those who already know God personally but want to know Him better.

But perhaps you do not yet know God in a personal way through His Son. You may think of yourself as a Christian only because you were taken to church as a child. Or you may take comfort from the fact that you were baptized as an infant and confirmed.

Family and church connections are an important part of religious life. But these experiences don't make a person a Christian.

Centuries ago, a religious leader named Nicodemus approached Jesus to find answers to his own spiritual questions. Nicodemus said, "We know that You are a teacher come from God; for no one can do these signs that You do unless God is with him" (Jn. 3:2).

Jesus' response seems surprisingly unrelated to Nicodemus' comments: "Jesus answered and said to him, 'Most assuredly, I say to you, unless one is born again, he cannot see the kingdom of God" (v.3).

Their conversation underscored the contrast between physical life and spiritual life. In the Garden of Eden, when God began to fellowship with Adam in the cool of the day, Adam had not yet disobeyed God. He was in a state of complete innocence. But after Adam disobeyed God by eating of the forbidden fruit, a fundamental change took place. A great barrier to fellowship between God and man damaged their relationship. When God made Himself available for fellowship with Adam as He had done in the past, Adam expressed his awareness of his disobedience by hiding from God (Gen. 3:8-10).

Sin had created an insurmountable chasm where once there had been an intimate union between God and man. The same alienation has persisted since that fateful day. All of us were made for fellowship with our Creator, but we have chosen to go our own way. The Bible says that "all we like sheep have gone astray; we have turned, every one, to his own way" (Isa. 53:6).

The tragic result of this rebellion against God is spiritual death. Adam was told that on the day he ate of the tree of the knowledge of good and evil he would surely die (Gen. 2:16-17). Adam ate of the forbidden fruit and at that moment he died spiritually. Although he lived on physically for many years, his ability to fellowship with God had been damaged by the consequences of sin.

That's why Jesus' words to Nicodemus were such good news. Jesus told him that each of us can be made alive again on the inside. God's Holy Spirit can come inside us and restore our fellowship with God. But how does this happen?

Pascal, the great mathematician, said that inside every human heart is a God-shaped vacuum that can only be filled with the person of Jesus Christ. The Lord is eager to forgive your sin, restore your fellowship with God, and give you the gift of eternal life. But there are some biblical requirements.

First, we must admit that we are sinners and cannot save ourselves. The Bible tells us that "all have sinned and fall short of the glory of God" (Rom. 3:23).

Second, we need to recognize the seriousness of our sin. Our human tendency is to rationalize and grade on a curve by comparing ourselves to others. But God sets a standard of perfection in which no one can please Him based on self-effort. The Bible says that "our righteousnesses are like filthy rags" (Isa. 64:6).

"The wages of sin is death, but the gift of God is eternal life in Christ Jesus our Lord" (Rom. 6:23). The good news is that Christ suffered the consequences of our sin, making it possible for us to have eternal fellowship with Him. The apostle Paul wrote, "God demonstrates His own love toward us, in that while we were still sinners, Christ died for us" (Rom. 5:8). This means that Jesus Christ, who never did anything wrong, gave His own life on the cross so that the penalty of sin could be paid and His righteousness applied to us (2 Cor. 5:21).

Third, it's not enough just to know that Christ died for us. We need to act on this by receiving Him as Savior and Lord. The Bible says, "As many as received Him, to them He gave the right to become children of God, to those who believe in His name" (Jn. 1:12).

Are you ready to make that decision? If you are, you can go to Jesus in prayer and share with Him your desire to receive forgiveness for sin and the start of an eternal relationship with Him.

"Jesus, I admit that I am a sinner. Thank You for dying on the cross to pay the penalty for my sin. I now receive You as my Savior and Lord. Take control of my life and make me the kind of person You want me to be. Amen."

Did you pray that prayer? If you did, you can have the assurance that Christ is in your life. The apostle John wrote, "These things I have written to you who believe in the name of the Son of God, that you may know that you have eternal life" (1 Jn. 5:13).

The devotional time that this chapter has talked about will now take on new meaning. Jesus Christ looks forward to spending time with you, and you will want to spend time with Him.

TWO

Jesus' Blueprint
For Prayer

One of the biggest problems in our relationship with God is thinking that we can depend on Him on our own terms. This independent dependence often shows up in the way we pray. While most people do pray, relatively few people pray to God on His terms.

This chapter is about praying the way God wants us to pray. The Lord's Prayer, one of the most familiar of all prayers, has been much repeated but little understood. Haddon Robinson, the featured teacher on RBC's *Discover The Word* daily radio program, cuts through the confusion and shows us that Jesus gave us a blueprint for prayer that is just as relevant today as it was 2,000 years ago.

MARTIN R. DE HAAN II

Jesus' Blueprint
for Prayer

I admire men and women who give prayer high priority in their lives. Frankly, prayer has proved to be the most demanding discipline of my life. At different times I have found it strenuous, boring, frustrating, and confusing. Over the years a solid prayer-life has been more intermittent than persistent. Occasionally I have grabbed hold of the hem of the garment, only to discover I could not sustain the grip. Out of my experience I have learned that you cannot simply "say your prayers." Prayer, real prayer, is tough, hard business.

To admit my lifelong struggle with prayer is something I do with great uneasiness. In the life of Jesus, prayer was the work, and ministry was the prize. For me, prayer serves as preparation for the battle, but for Jesus, it was the battle itself. Having prayed, He went about His ministry as an honor student might go to receive a reward, or as a marathon runner, having run the race, might accept the gold medal.

Where was it that Jesus sweat great drops of blood? Not in Pilate's Hall, nor on His way to Golgotha. It was in the Garden of Gethsemane. There He "offered up prayers and supplications, with vehement cries and tears to Him who was able to save Him from death" (Heb. 5:7). Had I been there and witnessed that struggle, I would have worried about the future. "If He is so broken up when all He is doing is praying," I might have said, "what will He do when He faces a real crisis? Why can't He approach this ordeal with the calm confidence of His three sleeping friends?" Yet, when the test came, Jesus walked to the cross with courage, and His three friends fell apart and fell away.

In Luke 11, after Jesus had spent time praying, one of His disciples asked Him, "Lord, teach us to pray, as John also taught his disciples." Two things are worth noting about the request. First, one section of John the Baptist's curriculum in disciple-making focused on teaching his followers to pray. Second, that was what Jesus' men asked Him to do for them. They had been with Him now for over 2 years. They had front seats when He taught and preached. They witnessed His miracles. Yet, as far as we know, they never took Him aside and asked, "Lord, teach us to preach," or "Lord, show us how to minister." They did come and request, "Teach us to pray."

We usually ask an expert to give us the best he has to offer. When we're with a successful banker, we ask, "Teach us to invest." From a gifted scholar we request, "Teach us to do research." To a professional golfer we say, "Teach us to putt." Jesus' disciples asked Him, "Teach us to pray."

Because prayer was central to His ministry, He wanted it to be vital in theirs, so He responded by giving them what is commonly called "The Lord's Prayer." Actually, the prayer is misnamed because the Lord Himself could not have prayed this prayer. As the Son of God without sin, He could not have joined in the petition, "Forgive us our sins." Perhaps the prayer should be labeled, "The Disciples' Prayer," since it is a primer on prayer for people like us. It serves us in praying as an outline serves a minister when he preaches a sermon or as a blueprint serves a builder when he constructs a building. It guides us as we go.

The skeleton of the prayer given to us by Luke opens with an address to God: "Father." The prayer then has two major sections. First, we are to talk to the Father about the Father—His person, His program, and His purpose: "Hallowed be Your Name," "Your kingdom come," "Your will be done." Then we speak to the Father about His family—the children's need for provision, pardon, and protection: "Give us day by day our daily bread," "Forgive us our sins, for we also forgive everyone who is indebted to us," and "Do not lead us into temptation."

While I still have courses to take in the School of Prayer, this model prayer of Jesus has ordered my prayer-life. Of course, you may deserve high grades in the subject. But if not, perhaps you can pick up some pointers that will teach you to pray.

GOD'S PATERNITY:
"Our Father"

At the outset we need to know who it is that we are praying to. According to Jesus, when we come to the God of the universe in prayer, we can call Him Father. Bound up in the word *Father* is a compact summary of the entire Christian faith. It is the answer to the philosopher Lessing's question, "Is the universe friendly?" When Christians bow before God and call

Him "Father," they are acknowledging that at the heart of the universe there is not only ultimate power but ultimate love.

But not everyone can call God "Father." It is Jesus who taught us to pray that way. He alone guarantees that we can enter into a relationship with God and become members of His family. He is our Father and we are His children.

There are some who hold to a view called the "Fatherhood of God and the brotherhood of man." This does not reflect the teaching of the Bible, however. It's true that God is the Creator of all, and in that sense everyone is "the offspring of God" (Acts 17:29). But the relationship that a creature has with his Creator is not the relationship of the Father to His children. The relationship that we have with God as our Father comes only through our relationship with Jesus Christ. John 1:12 says:

As many as received Him [Christ], to them He gave the right to become children of God, even to those who believe in His name.

It is a wonderful privilege to be able to call God "Father"—a privilege we easily take for granted. In the Old Testament, the people of God did not individually address Him as Father. The word *Father* for God was rarely used, and when it was it always referred to the relationship of God to the nation of Israel. As far as we know, none of the outstanding Old Testament saints— Abraham, Joseph, Moses, David, Daniel—ever fell to his knees in the solitude of his chambers and dared to address God as his Father. Yet in the New Testament, at least 275 times, that is how we are instructed to speak to God. Because of Jesus' death and resurrection, when we come to the sovereign majesty of the universe, the word that should fall readily from our lips is *Father*.

The address, "Our Father in heaven," as given in The Lord's Prayer, not only recognizes the intimacy that we have with God as our Father but it also speaks of the awe we should have as we come to Him in prayer. Jesus is saying that this One to whom we come as Father is the sovereign God of heaven, the God of all power, the God of all authority.

To the early Jewish Christians, having a proper awe of God was probably easier than understanding their intimacy with God. Unfortunately in our day, the pendulum has swung to the other extreme. God is often referred to in terms that are anything but awe-inspiring. I cannot conceive of the psalmist saying, "I may not know the answers, but I know the Answer Man." I cannot imagine the men and women of the Bible talking about "the big Man upstairs." To say that God is our Father does not imply that God is a great, big, huggable teddy bear.

The Bible keeps the tension between intimacy and awe. The writer of Hebrews said:

Let us therefore come boldly to the throne of grace, that we may obtain mercy and find grace to help in time of need (4:16).

The fact that we come to a throne should fill us with awe. But because it is a throne of *grace,* it is approachable. The sovereign, almighty God of the universe has allowed us, because of Jesus Christ, to approach Him in prayer and address Him as Father.

GOD'S PERSON:
"Hallowed Be Your Name"

When we pray, Jesus told us to say, "Our Father in heaven, hallowed be Your name" (Lk. 11:2). In Hebrew thought, a name was extremely significant. Parents did not name their children because they thought their initials would look good on luggage. They didn't choose a name because it reminded them of their Aunt Hilda or their Uncle Harry. Parents chose names for their children, hoping that the name would embody the personality, characteristics, or character that they wanted to see developed in the child.

Early American Puritans did that. They gave their daughters names like Silence, Charity, Hope, Love, and Patience. They hoped that the child would live up to her name as she grew up. We also see this in the New Testament. In times of crisis, when someone's life or outlook changed, often his name was changed to match. When Jesus got hold of Peter, his name was Simon. He was a shifty, sandy, undependable fellow. But Jesus changed his name to Peter, which means "rock." When Jesus renamed Peter, it took a while for him to live up to his new name—to change shifting sand into rock.

This practice of renaming was seen in more recent times when the cardinal of Poland became the pope. He changed his name to John Paul II because he wanted his life to embody the virtues of his predecessors, John XXIII, Paul VI, and John Paul I. He chose the name to personify what he wanted to be.

In Psalm 9:10 we read, "Those who know Your name will put their trust in You." The psalmist was not claiming that those who could pronounce God's name would trust in Him. He was saying that those who knew God's character and His power would put their trust in Him. So when we pray, "hallowed be Your name," we are talking about the character and person of God. To hallow means "to sanctify, to set apart, to make special." The opposite of *hallow* is "to profane, to disgrace, to besmirch the name." When we say, "hallowed be Your name," we are praying that God may be God to us, that He will be set apart in our prayers in such a way that it will be clear that we reverence God.

Sometimes our prayers are dangerously close to a blasphemous distortion. We often pray as if God were deaf and we have to shout to make Him hear us, as if He were ignorant and we have to explain to make Him understand, and as if He were calloused and we have to cajole to get Him to respond. Our prayers reveal a very inadequate idea of God.

Other times our prayers make it clear that many names on earth are more significant to us than the name of God in heaven. We can be more in awe of an employer, a professor, a loved one, a friend, or a government official than we are of the God in heaven. We can fear a fellow creature of earth more than we reverence and respect the God to whom we pray.

The petitions in this model prayer cover all that we

are to pray about. Whether we pray a short prayer or a long one, we will never pray more than what is contained here. We often pray for God to increase our devotion and depth of spiritual life, but none of the petitions found in this prayer are for personal holiness. The first step in spiritual growth is not to pray for inner feeling or inner change but that God will indeed be God in our lives. The focus of the spiritual life is not experience but God.

We have the command to be holy as He is holy because the spiritual life begins when we determine to allow God to be God in all aspects of life—personal, family, business, recreation—and to allow God to set us apart.

This focus on Him should be true not only in our own inner life but also in our prayers for others. We should not pray primarily that others will be delivered from sin but that they will come to know God. The ultimate goal of evangelism is not only that people will be won to Jesus Christ, but that people in the world who profane the name of God will come to understand who He really is—the God of holiness, grace, and righteousness. And out of that understanding, they will hallow His name. That is the essence of evangelism—people everywhere allowing God to be God in their lives.

GOD'S PROGRAM:
"Your Kingdom Come"

The second request that we direct to the Father about the Father is not only devoted to the person of God but also to the program of God. The second request is "Your kingdom come." Jesus was speaking here about His future messianic reign on the earth. All through Scripture, the story of the Bible looks forward to the return of the Messiah, Jesus Christ, who will rule in righteousness when the kingdom of this world will become the kingdom of our God and of His Christ (Rev. 11:15).

This concern for God's rule on the earth is basic to our view of history. Joseph Wittig once noted that a person's biography should begin not with his birth but with his death. He argued that we measure the contribution of life not by its beginning but by its end. That's how we should think about history. Any thoughtful person wonders, *Is history going anyplace? Is it simply a wheel that moves round and round and never touches the ground? Is it simply a cycle of repeated events headed for no destination except perhaps oblivion?* Some people shrug off history as a tale told by an idiot, scrawled on the walls of an insane asylum. Edward Gibbon referred to history as "little more than the register of crimes, follies, and misfortunes of mankind." Henry Ford summed up history as "bunk." Ralph Waldo Emerson dismissed history as "the biographies of a few great men."

In the witness of the Bible, however, history is "His story," and history is headed somewhere—the return of Jesus Christ. The Bible anticipates that day when the angels and the redeemed will sing together. Before us shines that light, and the darker the age, the brighter seems the glow.

So, when we pray, "Your kingdom come," we look toward that glad time when God's messianic kingdom prophesied throughout the Old Testament will be established by Jesus' return to earth. As we pray, we direct our gaze to the day when the kingdom of this world will become the kingdom of our God and of His Christ. We look forward to the climax of history when God's will shall be done on earth as it is in heaven.

When we pray, "Your kingdom come," though, we also ask for something else. We plead that on the small bit of earth we occupy now, we shall submit our will to God's will. If we long for the time in the future when Christ's kingdom will be established on earth—enough to pray sincerely for it—then we must be willing that all of the little kingdoms that matter too much to us will be pulled down. If we want God's rule over all men and women at some future time, then it follows that we desire that He will work His will out in our lives now.

When we pray, "Your kingdom come," we acknowledge God's right to rule all people, including us. Unless I am sufficiently concerned about God's sovereignty to make my life His throne, and make it my daily purpose to bring every individual whose life I touch into willing and glad submission to Him, I cannot pray these words with integrity. We dare not pray for His rule over others unless we honestly desire His rule over us.

When I was in my twenties, I used to hear sermons in which I was exhorted to desire the second coming of Christ. Well, I wanted Him to come, but not immediately. I had some things I wanted to do before He came back. I wanted to get married, to have children, and to establish a ministry. After I got all that done, it would be all right for Him to return. As I was thinking about this recently, it occurred to me that I no longer have any plans that the coming of Jesus Christ would interrupt. Nothing now takes precedence over His coming. And that is as it should be in all of our lives. That is what it means to pray, "Your kingdom come."

GOD'S PURPOSE:
"Your Will Be Done"

We are to pray for the person of God, that His name will be hallowed; for the program of God, that His kingdom will come; and for the purpose of God, that His will will be done on earth as it is in heaven.

Praying for His will to be done provides a foundation for our prayers. We are basically asking that God's will be done in our lives and in the world. We often get it upside down, though, and pray as if we expect God to change the way He is running the universe because we have given Him our petitions. At our worst, we treat God like a genie in a lamp. When we rub it and make a wish, we expect God to change the universe to give us what we want.

> For us to do God's will on earth as it is in heaven, we must go against the current.

We must recognize the importance of conforming our will to His will. We shouldn't pray for something and then say, "if it be Your will," if we don't really mean it. These words aren't something to tack on to the end of a prayer as a loophole, as an "out," so that if God doesn't give us what we want we won't be embarrassed. Prayer is not getting God to do *my* will; it is asking that *God's* will be done in my life, my family, my business, and in my relationships, as it is done in heaven.

When the Bible gives us glimpses of heaven, we see that the angels stand ready to do His bidding. In heaven, all the hosts of glory respond to His will. In the universe, all the galaxies and all their stars and planets move according to His design. It seems that only here on this third-rate planet, this dirty little tennis ball that we call earth, is there a pocket of rebellion.

For us to live according to God's will on earth as it is done in heaven is to do so in enemy territory. To live in a realm that is controlled by Satan is to recognize that this world is no friend of God's. For us to do God's will on earth as it is in heaven, we must go against the current. When we pray, "Your will be done on earth as it is in heaven," we are praying for our friends, our families, our society, but above all for ourselves.

When Beethoven's body was exhumed 42 years after his death, he was found with his arms up and his fists clenched in defiance. Apparently, someone had buried him in a way that revealed his attitude. At the age of 30, Beethoven had become deaf and remained that way until his death 26 years later. He died an angry and bitter man because he felt that God had hemmed him in. Although he might have prayed for God's will to be done, he would have done so in grim resignation. It is possible to pray for God's will while resenting that God is God. Many people despise God because He has not made them master of their fate, captain of their soul, or rulers of their own destiny. But those of us who know God as Father and have a relationship with Him, who know that the heart of the Almighty is not only righteous and holy but also gracious and kind, can know that all things will work together for good to those who love God.

And so we can pray that His name will be hallowed, that He will be God to us, that His kingdom will be established on earth, that every knee will bow and every tongue confess that Jesus Christ is Lord, and that His will will be done on earth as it is in heaven.

GOD'S PROVISION:
"Give Us Our Daily Bread"

When Jesus taught us to pray, He gave us a comprehensive blueprint to follow. The first three requests deal with God's glory. The last three requests deal with the family. While the petitions to the Father talk about "Your name," "Your kingdom," and "Your will," the last three requests have to do with us: "Give us," "forgive us," and "lead us."

German theologian Helmut Thielicke points out that the whole of life is captured in the rainbow of these requests: "Great things and small things; spiritual things and material things; inward things and outward things— there is nothing that is not included in this prayer."

Adlai Stevenson once remarked, "Understanding human needs is half the job of meeting them." Perhaps the other half is the ability to meet them. God scores on both counts. Because God understands our needs and can truly meet them, Jesus said that we are to pray to the Father about them. After praying about that which is cosmic and eternal, we are to pray about that which is temporal.

When Jesus said, "Give us today our daily bread," He was not suggesting a trip to the supermarket for Wonder Bread. He was making the point that it is okay and right to pray for our daily needs. After all, we cannot really serve His kingdom and do His will unless we have the strength we need for today. So it is proper to ask God for a job in order to have money for food. It is appropriate to appeal to God for the clothes we need to work on the job in order to have the food. It is okay to ask for transportation to get us to the job so that we may earn the bread. God knows our needs, and He is concerned about them.

We are often tempted not to bother asking God for food. "Don't pray for groceries," we insist. "Get out and hustle." In fact, some of the church fathers spiritualized the bread to refer to the bread served at communion. They did this, understandably, because after praying for God's glory, it seemed too earthly to switch to something as mundane as groceries.

Yet, "daily bread" means exactly what it says. The word *bread* refers to the food that sustains our bodies. In the larger sense, of course, bread refers to all that we must have to live. Our Father in heaven concerns

Himself with the items on a grocery list. Food for our next meal matters to Him.

The focus of the request is for *daily* bread. The word translated *daily* bewildered scholars for centuries. This is the only place that word occurred inside or outside the Bible. Then a few years ago, an archaeologist dug up a papyrus fragment that contained a housewife's shopping list. Next to several items the woman had scribbled this word for *daily*. It probably meant, "enough for the coming day." The phrase should be translated, "Give us today bread enough for tomorrow." When prayed in the morning, it is a prayer for the needs in the hours ahead. Prayed in the evening, it is a request for the needs of the next day. The implication is, of course, that God will supply what we need to honor Him and do His will.

In our culture, with its freezers and refrigerators, we seldom purchase food for a single day. We store up food in such abundance that we mutter only thoughtless words of thanks as we eat. We hardly acknowledge that the meal we eat or the clothes we wear have come from the Father's hand.

Jesus does not invite us to ask for everything in the Neiman Marcus catalog, or for a Lincoln Continental, or Gucci shoes. Pray for bread—the necessities for life, not the luxuries. Ask for bread, not cake. Nor are we invited to request supplies for years to come. We are to ask for the essentials to take us through tomorrow.

Notice also that when we pray, "Give us our daily bread," we ask for others in the family as well as ourselves. If I pray this prayer in sincerity, it delivers me from selfishness and hoarding. If the Father supplies me with two loaves and my brother or sister with none, I understand that God has indeed answered our prayers. My extra loaf is not for storing, but for sharing.

God wants to free us up. We can bring our small requests to God. We can place before Him our need for bread, a coat, a pair of shoes—all those items that matter to us. If we need them, then they matter to our heavenly Father as well.

GOD'S PARDON:
"Forgive Us Our Sins"

Superficially, men and women don't seem to worry much about their sins. Walter Horton speaks to our condition in his book, *The Challenge Of Our Culture*: "Modern man is certainly worried about something—worried nearly to death. And an analysis of his behavior shows him so feverishly trying to avoid looking God in the eye that it must have something to do with the fear of how he must look standing before God in that position." A cartoon in the morning newspaper pictures a psychologist listening to a patient: "Mr. Figby," he says, "I think I can explain your feelings of guilt. You're guilty!"

After we ask the Father for provision, we ask for pardon: "Forgive us our sins." "Forgive" follows "give." Jesus links the two petitions, "Give us our daily bread" with "Forgive us our sins, for we also forgive everyone who is indebted to us." In that way when we think of our need for food, we will recognize our need for pardon as well. Also, as we confess our guilt, we consider how we have handled our relationships with others.

Augustine labeled this request "the terrible petition" because if we pray, "Forgive us our sins, for we also forgive everyone who is indebted to us," and at the same time harbor an unforgiving spirit, we are actually asking God not to forgive us.

When John Wesley served as a missionary to the American colonies, he had a difficult time with General James Oglethorpe. The general was known for his pride and harshness. One time Oglethorpe declared, "I never forgive." Wesley replied, "Then, Sir, I hope you never sin!"

> "Modern man is certainly worried about something— worried nearly to death."
> —WALTER HORTON

Think of how the confession of sin works. If I honestly pray for forgiveness, then I revise my estimate of myself downward on the scale, and I admit my own sin and guilt. If I see the pollution of my own life, then I see the sins of others in a different light. Without that, I can regard myself as so important, so dignified, so honorable that it would be unthinkable to forgive anyone who dared offend someone as righteous as I. That is self-righteousness. To squeeze pardon from a self-righteous prig is harder than squeezing apple juice from a stone slab. It's simply not in such a person to forgive.

What an unforgiving person actually prays is this: "Deal with me as I have dealt with others." Kent Hughes spells that out in his study on The Lord's Prayer: "I beseech You, Lord, deal with me as I deal with my neighbor. He has been ungrateful to me (though not one-hundredth as ungrateful as I have been to You), yet I will not overlook his ingratitude. Deal with me, Lord, as I do him."

Or this: "I nurse every little incident in which she mistreats me. Deal with me, Lord, as I deal with her."

Or this: "I cannot wait to pay him back for the hurt he has done to me. Deal with me, Lord, as I deal with him."

If you honestly know God as your Father, you are part of the forgiven fellowship. While you may find it hard to forgive some particularly damaging thing done to you, your own sin against God—for which you ask forgiveness—makes offenses done against you much more trivial. How in the name of grace and common sense can we ask God whose name is holy to forgive us when we, as sinners, refuse to forgive others? Our forgiveness does not cause God to forgive us. It is evidence that we have entered into God's forgiveness. Those who live in the relief of God's pardon find it easier to forgive those who offend them.

To sin is human, to forgive divine. We are never closer to God's grace than when we admit our sin and cry out for pardon. We are never more like God than when, for Christ's sake, we extend forgiveness fully and freely to those who have sinned against us.

GOD'S PROTECTION:
"Do Not Lead Us Into Temptation"

A young woman in a shopping mall sported a T-shirt that proclaimed, "Lead me not into temptation—I can find it myself." She wanted people to chuckle as she passed, but her one-liner raised a question. What are we praying for when we ask, "Do not lead us into temptation"?

Why should we have to ask God not to lead us into temptation? To ask Him to keep us out of temptation would be more understandable. Professor D. A. Carson suggests that Jesus is using a figure of speech called a *litotes*, which expresses something positive by negating its opposite. For example, if I say, "This is no small matter," I mean it is a big matter. When we pray, "Lead us not into temptation," then, we are really crying out, "Keep me away from temptation." We are praying, "Don't let Satan ambush us. Don't let the foe of our souls catch us in his trap." We are recognizing that God has the power to lead us past all the lures to sin that threaten us; and we are asking, "If the opportunity to sin presents itself, grant that I will not have the desire. If the desire springs up within me, grant that I will not have the opportunity."

Let's face it. We seldom want to be delivered from temptation. It promises too much fun. Some wag has said, "Don't resist temptation. It may go away and not come back." Temptation stirs the blood and inflames the imagination. If we were revolted by it, it would not be temptation at all. Occasionally we see where temptation will take us and we may cry out for deliverance. Usually, though, temptation doesn't seem very bad, so we play with it, flirt with it, and invite it into our lives. When we pray about our sins, it's not temptation that bothers us; it's the consequence of our disobedience that we want removed.

In the context of this prayer, however, we are not merely asking God to keep us from being naughty boys and girls. The work of Satan threatens more severe danger than that. We are surrounded by seductions to live life apart from God. In our ambitions and in our successes we are tempted to honor our own names, to build our own kingdoms, to take credit for baking our own bread, and to deny our need for forgiving grace. The enemy of our souls wants us to run away from God. Only God can make us see sin for what it is. If temptation brought chains to bind us, we might resist it on our own.

> Let's face it.
> We seldom
> want to be
> delivered from
> temptation.
> It promises
> too much fun.

Instead, it brings flowers and perfume, offers life and cheer, and promises good times and satisfaction. It bribes us with wealth and popularity and entices us with promises of prosperity and unbounded freedom. Only God can keep us from its charms.

The Lord's Prayer reminds us to fear the strategies of Satan. Years ago Helmut Thielicke said of postwar occupied Germany, "There is a dark, mysterious, spellbinding figure at work. Behind the temptations stands the tempter, behind the lie stands the liar, behind all the dead and bloodshed stands the 'murderer from the beginning.' "

When we pray "Deliver us from the evil one," we recognize Satan's power, affirm our weakness, and plead for the greater power of God.

GOD'S PREEMINENCE:
"The Kingdom, The Power, And The Glory"

The Lord's Prayer, as we commonly recite it, concludes with a trumpet blast of praise: "For Yours is the kingdom and the power and the glory forever. Amen." Since those words seem like an appropriate and fitting way for the prayer to end, it is somewhat unsettling to discover that the sentence does not appear in the earliest and best manuscripts of either Matthew or Luke. Evidently, the doxology was not part of the prayer as Jesus originally gave it. In fact, it appears for the first time in the second and third centuries.

Yet the prayer demands a conclusion. Otherwise it stops with the threat of temptation and the warning that the evil one has set his snares for us. When Christians in the young church offered up this prayer to the Father, rather than finish on a cold and frightening note, they added this affirmation of praise.

While this doxology may not have been given directly by Jesus, it can claim broad biblical support. After King David assembled the building materials for the future temple, he declared:

Yours, O Lord, is the greatness, the power and the glory,
the victory and the majesty; . . . Yours is the kingdom
(1 Chr. 29:11).

Echoes of this doxology vibrate at the end of time
in the chant of the four living creatures:

Blessing and honor and glory and power be to Him who
sits on the throne, and to the Lamb, forever and ever!
(Rev. 5:13).

The affirmation makes a fitting conclusion to the
prayer:

For Yours is the kingdom and the power and the glory
forever. Amen (Mt. 6:13).

But is that true? Does the kingdom belong to God?
Not according to the newspapers. There the capital of
the kingdom may be in Washington or London or
Moscow, not in heaven. Is His the power? Not according to Rabbi Harold Kushner, who argues in *When*
Bad Things Happen To Good People, that while God is
all-loving, some evil events lie beyond His control. Is
His the glory? Not according to the builders and
shapers of technology who sing, "Glory to men on earth
as we see whose buildings can go the highest."

This doxology, however, is not an assumption that
we must accept in order to pray, but rather a confidence
to which repeated prayer draws us. When God's kingdom and the dignity of God's name get first emphasis in
our lives, then money and bottom lines stop bringing us
anxiety and strife. Then, and only then, as we ask for
daily bread, we recognize that apart from God full

stomachs often come with empty hearts. Through prayer we experience that God actually forgives our sins—not simply shuts His eyes to our disobedience—and provides us with the power to forgive others and lead us away from Satan's traps. In a life of prayer we discover a Father rich and generous and inexhaustible beyond all measure: His is the kingdom and the power and the glory.

Not only do we bless God when we witness what He does through answered prayer but we also praise God because on our knees we can catch a glimpse by faith of what He will ultimately accomplish. We make all our prayers in the light of eternity. In the long-range view we discover that though wicked men and women fight against Christ's rule, His kingdom waits as the sun waits for the clouds and darkness to melt away. In the eternal perspective, while the Love which lay in a manger and hung on a Roman execution rack looks fragile, we see in it the power which endures and ultimately triumphs. As presidents and kings display their glory, we know they form a passing parade. Yesterday's empires are today's history lessons and tomorrow's archaeological digs.

Over the rubble of man's little kingdoms shines the glory of God. When we pray as we ought, we affirm God's majesty, trumpet His power, and, through the answers to our prayer, display His glory.

> The doxology is not an assumption that we must accept in order to pray, but rather a confidence to which repeated prayer draws us.

Why Do We Pray?

Any thoughtful person wrestling with prayer asks, "Why pray at all?" Is the basic purpose of prayer to get things from God? Certainly the Bible assures us that God hears us and, in response, gives us what we need. But is that the basic reason Jesus taught us to pray?

George MacDonald offered this rationale for prayer: "What if God knows prayer to be the thing we need first and most? What if the main object in God's idea of prayer is a supplying of our great, our endless need—the need of Himself? . . . Hunger may drive the runaway child home, and he may or may not be fed at once, but he needs his parents more than his dinner. Communion with God is the one need of the soul beyond all other need. Prayer is the beginning of that communion, of talking with God, a coming-to-one with Him, which is the sole end of prayer, yea, of existence itself. . . . We must ask that we may receive, but that we should receive what we ask in respect to our lower needs is not God's end in making us pray. He could give us everything without that. To bring His child to His knee, God withholds that men may ask."

God wants us for Himself. He desires communion with us. His purpose in prayer is not to make us sit up and beg. He wants us to know Him. Prayer is His method to accomplish that.

I used to play a game with my two children when

they were young. I would clutch some pennies in my hand and allow them to pry open my fingers to get the coins. My children would sit on my lap and work feverishly to get the money. Once they captured the coins, they would scream with delight and jump down to treasure their prize. I loved having my youngsters laugh and play while sitting on my lap. The pennies were insignificant.

When we pray, we often concentrate on the gifts in God's hand and ignore the hand of God Himself. We pray fervently for the new job, or for the return of health. When we gain the prize, we are delighted. And then we have little more to do with God. If we are only after the coins, God's hand serves only as a way to pay the rent, heal the sickness, or get through the crisis. After the need has been met, the hand itself means little to us.

While God in His grace does give good gifts to His children, He offers us more than that. He offers us Himself. Those who are merely satisfied with the trinkets in the Father's hand miss the best reward of prayer—the reward of communicating and communing with the God of the universe.

Using The Blueprint

To really learn about prayer, you must pray. Take it seriously and carve out some time each day to pray. Jesus gave us a blueprint for prayer—use it that way. Begin by praying, "Our Father in heaven." Let your mind focus on what it means to talk to the God of the universe as Father. Then pray to the Father about the Father. Pray about His person, "hallowed be Your name." Pray about His program, "Your kingdom come." And pray about His purpose, "Your will be done."

Then pray to the Father about the family. Pray for provision, "Give us our daily bread." Pray for pardon, "And forgive us our sins." And pray for protection, "Lead us not into temptation."

If you let this prayer serve as your blueprint, you will discover that its elements have a purifying effect on what you pray for. You won't be able to pray for things that would exalt your name, advance your kingdom, or promote your will. To ask for daily bread if you're living in defiance would be like a traitor asking for strength to betray his country. You won't be able to ask God to forgive you when you are not willing to forgive someone else. And to ask God for His protection from the evil one would be contradictory if you are cultivating temptations.

Prayer is hard work, but our communication with God is essential to our spiritual well-being.

THREE

Praying With Confidence

OVERCOMING DISAPPOINTMENT IN PRAYER

D isappointment has a way of turning prayers into silence. It can be hard to pray when you are bitter and angry toward people you believe are ruining your life. It can be even harder to pray when you feel that God Himself has let you down.

God understands our feelings. Yet He has made a way for us to come with confidence to His throne of grace. In the following pages, David Egner offers help to those who have lost confidence in God and in their own ability to know that He is listening when they pray.

MARTIN R. DE HAAN II

The Trouble With Prayer

In front of me sat a group of adult singles who were gathered to do a study on prayer. I handed out a sheet of paper that began with this statement: "When it comes to prayer, I _____." They were to fill in the blank.

How would you respond? It might be helpful for you to do just that. Complete this sentence:

When it comes to prayer, I _____.

When I tabulated what the group had written, the results fell into these categories:

- "I don't pray enough."
- "I don't know what to pray."
- "I don't know if prayer does any good."

I've found such answers common. While a few speak glowingly of the ease with which they slip in and out of conversations with God, more seem to view prayer as a struggle that is sometimes won but more often lost.

It is understandable that prayer would not always come easily. Rightly understood, it is not just emotion addressed to God. It is also an expression of faith that is often weak and small. It is a weapon of spiritual warfare that is used to fight for contested ground. It is a reflection of a relationship with God that is often disrupted and strained by our own ignorance, inattention, and insensitivity. It is an expression of confidence in God that is often replaced by feelings of disappointment.

Early in our Christian walk, we pray with high expectations. We assume that God will give us the deepest desires of our heart, and that through prayer we will experience the closeness and happiness we long for. With our confidence in God, we believe that we will rise above any problem.

Then we ask God for something important to us and we don't get it. We assure ailing friends that we are praying for their recovery, but they don't get better. We pray in the presence of our family for a solution to problems that are affecting them, only to be left waiting for months and months while God seems to ignore us. We plead earnestly and often for our loved ones' spiritual restoration, but they remain cold toward God.

Slowly, disappointment forms. We lose our enthusiasm for prayer. Soon we're praying only at mealtimes. We go through a phase when we won't bring anything we really care about to the Lord because we can't take another rejection. We stop communicating with God.

Think about your prayer relationship with God. If you've stopped growing in prayer, is it because of honest disappointment?

Disappointment With God

"I asked and believed that God was going to heal my daughter. But she lost her fight with cancer anyway. I'm brokenhearted and confused."

Disappointment With Others

"I have a hard time praying when I am so angry with people who are ruining my life."

Disappointment With Ourselves

"I've wanted to pray. I've looked forward to it. I've had the best of intentions. But I just haven't been able to get around to it."

It takes faith and courage to work through a disrupted human relationship. It's the same in our relationship with God. The first step is to admit the problem. Then we must work past the disappointment and regain our confidence in God. The remainder of this study can help build that confidence.

But before we go on, let me speak personally. I know a little of what it means to be disappointed with the turns and twists of life. Sometimes the most disturbing experiences have involved what God has allowed in the lives of those closest to my heart. One of those times involved the health of a dear grandson. Nathan was born with an immune deficiency. His tiny body had no mechanism for fighting disease. In the first few years of his life, we watched helplessly as he struggled through a series of upper respiratory infections. God didn't seem to be answering our pleas.

As a family we were frightened. Could we trust God even if He didn't answer our prayers for this one so dear to our hearts?

Doctors told us that the immune system in 60 percent of these children "kicks in" about the time they turn 3. While that information offered hope, it also left us with the realization that 40 percent do not develop defenses against infection. Time after time, I looked at that defenseless little body and prayed.

At first I was consumed by the "what ifs" of Nathan's condition. As time went on, the focus of my prayers changed. I was no longer as absorbed in the pain I was feeling. I found myself using fewer words. I wrestled, often in silence, on Nathan's behalf. Eventually I was saying simply, "God, do what's best. Only You know, and I trust You and Your goodness. I want so much for You to heal him. Yet, Your will be done."

About the time Nate turned 3, he began to have fewer infections. God mercifully let Nathan be one of the 60 percent who overcome immune deficiency.

Through such uncontrollable circumstances of life I have been learning to trust God in the school of prayer. Sometimes I have been grateful for His "yes." Sometimes I've seen the wisdom of a "no." Sometimes I've even learned to enjoy God in the process of waiting for His answer.

Yet I still find myself lapsing into the discouragement of circumstances. I find myself longing for the kind of power that would give me Elijah-like control over physical conditions (Jas. 5:16-18). What I've learned, however, is that real confidence in prayer isn't found by projecting my desires upon God. Instead, I have found confidence by learning some simple yet profound principles of prayer. They do not depend on our ability to be eloquent or spiritually insightful. They have ABC-like qualities that are learned in our Lord's school of prayer.

Returning To The Basics

APPROACH GOD
THROUGH A MEDIATOR

Mediation was God's idea. He knew we had a problem trusting Him. But He could not ignore what we were doing. So God offered mediation. To resolve the differences that had come between us, He sent One who could understand and be sympathetic to our condition while at the same time representing the interests of heaven.

This Mediator so identified with us and became so involved in our problems that He ended up crying out, "My God, My God, why have You forsaken Me?" (Mk. 15:34). Yet, 3 days after that inexpressible moment, it became clear that the Mediator had been victorious. Through His great sacrifice, our Mediator had removed the barrier that had disrupted our relationship with God.

We would still sin. We would still be blinded by our own desires and stubborn pride. We would still find ourselves filled with regret. We would still become confused about what God was doing in our lives. But never again would we have reason to doubt the Father's love for us. Never again could it be persuasively argued that the Father didn't care, that He wasn't touched by our problems, or that He had left us to die in our circumstances. Never again would we have to approach God in prayer without the assurance that He wanted to talk with us far more than we wanted to talk to Him.

Without this mediatorial work, we might have wondered if God would even listen to us when we prayed. We might assume from our circumstances that He didn't care. But now memory of what happened on the Mediator's cross can restore confidence in us whenever we approach God in prayer. Now we can take courage in the fact that we don't have to approach God in our own sin-stained reputation. We don't come to Him in our own name. We don't approach Him with our own carefully chosen words. We come to Him in the merits of the One who paid for all of our sins with His own blood. We come to God in the name and interests of His own and dearly loved Son, Jesus Christ.

Confidence In A Past Sacrifice

This manner of approach has always been in God's mind for us. Long before our Mediator's arrival, the design for such an approach to God was illustrated in the tabernacle and temple worship of Israel. For many centuries God had made it clear that His people must approach Him on the basis of a blood sacrifice. But only in the coming and suffering of Christ do we see that those sacrifices illustrated the violent suffering and death of God's own Son.

There was in the same temple, in a place that signified the very Presence of God, an altar of incense.

This burning incense, by its fragrance and ascending motion, symbolized prayers that please God. Significantly, this incense was lit by a coal from the altar of sacrifice (Ex. 30:7-10). In God's mind, there is a connection between the sacrifice and the prayers by which we approach Him.

This link between sacrifice and prayer is what our Mediator secured for us. He offered a sacrifice acceptable to God. Then He encouraged us to go into the presence of God in His own name. Of this basis for confidence, the author of Hebrews wrote:

Seeing then that we have a great High Priest who has passed through the heavens, Jesus the Son of God, let us hold fast our confession. For we do not have a High Priest who cannot sympathize with our weaknesses, but was in all points tempted as we are, yet without sin. Let us therefore come boldly to the throne of grace, that we may obtain mercy and find grace to help in time of need (Heb. 4:14-16).

Being in the presence of God is described in this passage as like being in a throne room. In Europe and the Middle East, the throne rooms of kings were ornately and elaborately decorated and filled with attendants. Common people felt inferior and intimidated—the very feelings we might have as we approach God in prayer. But through the mediation and understanding of Christ, we can walk confidently into the presence of God without feeling like an unwanted intruder. We come in the name and merits of the Son of God, and that gives us access to the

Father at any time. We have an invitation stamped with the royal seal to pray at any time, under any conditions, whatever our circumstances or needs, because this is a "throne of grace." Grace is undeserved kindness. Grace is unmerited assistance. This is the kind of help our Mediator has secured for us.

Confidence In A Present Advocate

There's more! We can come to "the throne of grace" with confidence in our Mediator because His work for us continues. Even now He is at the right hand of God interceding on our behalf (Rom. 8:34). On the merit of His sacrifice, the Lord Jesus is our Intercessor. He is with the Father in the throne room, speaking on our behalf. The apostle John expressed it this way:

> *If anyone sins, we have an Advocate with the Father, Jesus Christ the righteous. And He Himself is the propitiation [the atoning sacrifice] for our sins (1 John 2:1-2).*

Why do we hold back? How could we feel hesitant or unworthy to pray when Jesus Christ Himself, on the basis of His sacrifice, is right now with the Father interceding for us?

BE HONEST ABOUT
YOUR COMPLAINTS

God loves honest talk. Realism is at the heart of His own character. He hates darkness and deception. Darkness is the domain of His enemy. Therefore, a second essential to confidence in prayer is to learn to be honest about what is in our hearts. He can handle our complaints, our foolishness, our fears, and our failures. He won't be surprised or threatened by our anger, our confusion, or our childlike pleadings.

What does not please God are the cheap lies of flattery, ritual praise, and insincere words repeated over and over without regret for what is really happening in our own soul. We need to put away our practices of fearful coverup, our sophisticated deceit, and our formal language, and instead lay the foundation of truth as the basis for prayer.

Prayers filled with pious lies are unacceptable to God, and they do not reflect the true spirit of our own hearts. That is why, in order to enter the throne room of grace and begin to pray with confidence, we must learn to be truthful when we pray. To do this, we have to spend time in self-evaluation and confession of sin. We must tell God how we really feel about Him, about ourselves, about our problems with people, and about our needs, frustrations, desires, and painful memories. We must also be honest about our desire to know His will and make it our own. If we don't want to do His will, then that too must be brought to the light so we can ask God to help us overcome our rebellion and foolishness.

Confidence In God's Ability To Help Us Understand Ourselves

When we want to know the truth about ourselves, the Lord who knows our hearts will help us to see what is happening in us. The psalmist wrote, "O Lord, You have searched me and known me" (Ps. 139:1). David said to Solomon, "The Lord searches all hearts and understands all the intent of the thoughts" (1 Chr. 28:9).

The prayer of self-examination, when combined with the Scriptures, enables us to see what's really going on inside. The Bible shows us our deep-seated feelings and true motives. It takes us into the nooks and crannies where we hide old grudges and secret hatreds and bitter resentments. Through honest prayer we can bring these things to the surface, see them for what they really are, and ask God to help us deal with them.

Of this we can be confident: If we ask God to show us our hearts, He will do it. Perhaps not immediately, but over time and in His own way, the Lord will pull back the curtains of denial and repression and show us ourselves. And He will take good care of us while He's doing it.

- He might bring an old hurt to mind for us to deal with and forget.
- He might remind us of a promise we have not kept or a debt we have not paid.
- He might let us feel the hurt we gave to someone else, perhaps many years ago, and tell us to make it right.
- He might direct us to straighten out a misunderstanding or forgive someone.

Heart knowledge is a wonderful, liberating gift,

and it comes through being honest with the Lord in prayer.

Self-examination can also reveal the positive blessings in our lives. God is working in us and doing things for us all the time. He shows us His goodness, fills us with grace, helps us grow through adversity, sustains us through difficult circumstances, gives us ways to escape temptation, and grants us His peace. But when we're caught up in the details of life and distracted by responsibilities, we are sometimes oblivious to these things.

> **Prayers filled with pious lies are unacceptable to God.**

Confidence In God's Willingness To Forgive An Honest Heart

It was the bottom of the ninth inning and the score was tied. The opposing team had the bases loaded with two outs. A hard grounder was hit a little to the right of the rookie shortstop. It bounced off his glove. The run scored and the game was lost. He had made that play a thousand times before—but not that time.

That ballplayer could have done what a lot of us do. He could have claimed that the ball hit a rock and took a bad bounce. He could have blamed the sun or the wet grass. But he didn't. "I blew it," he said after the game. "I take responsibility. It was my fault."

We need that attitude toward God. When the Lord convicts us of sin, we need to admit it, confess it, and then believe in His willingness to forgive us.

Remember the story of David and Nathan? Corrupted by power, David turned the war over to his generals and stayed at home. He looked lustfully at a bathing Bathsheba, had her brought to the palace, committed adultery, then had her husband killed to cover up his sin. It appeared that he would get away with it—until he was confronted by Nathan the prophet with those undeniable words of condemnation, "You are the man!" (2 Sam. 12:7).

Finally, after days and probably many months of living in self-imposed darkness, David acknowledged his sin. His moving prayer of repentance is recorded in Psalm 51. "I acknowledge my transgressions," he confessed to the Lord, "and my sin is always before me. Against You, You only, have I sinned" (vv.3-4). David pleaded for a restoration of the joy he once had, and his prayer was answered by the forgiveness of God. The Bible, the Holy Spirit, and God's people serve as our Nathans today.

We live in a calloused world of hardened hearts and desensitized consciences. Lawyers can argue cases with skill and apparent sincerity even when they know the defendant is guilty. Sentences for horrible crimes are received without a sign of guilt or remorse. We are experts at denial and rationalization and finding someone else to blame.

How can we soften our hearts? We're so accustomed to an iron-shelled coldness. How do we get "a broken and a contrite heart" (Ps. 51:17) that is always accepted by the Lord? Ask for it. "Create in me a clean heart," we must plead. "Renew a steadfast spirit within me" (v.10). God will honor that prayer. He doesn't turn away when we pray, "God, be merciful to me a sinner!" (Lk. 18:13).

Confidence In God's Ability To Handle Our Complaints

Our human relationships are cluttered with disagreements, struggles, and conflict. If there are no conflicts in a relationship, a confrontation is probably being suppressed and postponed until the future. Friends and lovers talk about their negative feelings openly and work through their differences. That should also be true in our relationship with God. We are free to respectfully and reverently disagree, question, and even argue with Him in prayer.

> When the Lord convicts us of sin, we need to admit it, confess it, and believe in His willingness to forgive us.

Rabbi Joseph Telushkin writes of the need for honest confrontations with God as being a legacy of the Jewish people. In his book *Jewish Literacy*, he writes:

> [The] first instance of a human being arguing with God becomes a characteristic feature of the Hebrew Bible, and of Judaism in general. Hundreds of years after Abraham, the psalmist called out to God in anger and anguish: "Awake! Why do You sleep, O Lord? . . . Why do You hide Your face, and forget our affliction

and our oppression?" (Ps. 44:23-24; see Habakkuk 1:2 and the entire book of Job for other examples of prophets or righteous men questioning God's ways). The willingness to confront the Almighty stems from the belief that God, like man, has responsibilities, and deserves criticism when He fails to fulfill them. Elie Wiesel, a Jew who stands in this tradition, has declared: "The Jew may love God, or he may fight with God, but he may not ignore God."

This seems to have been Abraham's attitude. God was about to destroy the wicked city of Sodom. Abraham interceded with the Lord, asking that the city be spared if 50 righteous people could be found. They could not. So, step by step, Abraham pleaded with God to reduce the number to 10. But when 10 could not be found, Sodom was destroyed (Gen. 18:23-33).

Moses also disagreed with God. The Lord had performed miracle after miracle to deliver Israel from Egyptian bondage and provide for them in the wilderness. But while Moses was in the heights of Mount Sinai receiving the Law from the hand of the Lord, his countrymen were getting ready to give up on the One who had delivered them from Egypt. In violation of the first commandments God had given Moses, they made an idol of gold and used it as an excuse to indulge in the sexual abandon of pagan fertility worship. "Now therefore, let Me alone," God said to Moses, "that My wrath may burn hot against them and I may consume them" (Ex. 32:10). God even said He would start over again and make a great nation out of Moses.

Moses didn't want to give in. He pleaded with the Lord to spare Israel, "Why should the Egyptians speak, and say, 'He brought them out to harm them, to kill them in the mountains, and to consume them from the face of the earth'? Turn from Your fierce wrath, and

> **We are free to respectfully and reverently disagree, question, and even argue with God in prayer.**

relent from this harm to Your people" (v.12). God relented, and the Jews were spared (v.14).

Abraham and Moses are good examples for us. We too can clear the air with God. While still fearing God and remembering to reverence Him, we can:

- Ask Him why He's waiting so long to save our loved one.
- Express our anger and disappointment because our child was not spared.
- Pour out our frustration to Him because we haven't found a job yet.
- Cry out to Him because we are still childless.

Such complaints do not threaten God. He knows we will never find a moral weakness in Him. He encourages us to be honest with Him so that we can discover the thoughts and feelings that are in our hearts. Once we bring them to the light, we can ask God to help us deal with them.

Why are we so hesitant to be honest with God? Perhaps we're the kind of people who avoid all conflict. We won't even tell our loved ones or friends any of our negative feelings. Or we may think it would be a lack of faith to challenge God.

Many of us have accepted society's idea that struggle and love do not go together. We assume that a relationship is good only as long as there is peace and harmony. The fact remains that we struggle in relationships because we really do care. And finding the courage to struggle and take risks and confront is what strengthens and deepens all relationships. The same is true in our relationship with God. Like Jacob at Bethel, we do well to wrestle with God once in a while. It can bring us His blessing (Gen. 32:24-32).

Confidence In What God Wants For Us

The goal of the believer in Jesus Christ is to become one (in heart and agreement) with God. When we come to Him in prayer, we need to be honest with ourselves about whether our desires are His desires, whether our will is His will, whether our requests would be His requests.

How do we grow in this "oneness" with God? Certainly we can never share in His complete understanding of all things. Yet, as we pray for the daily needs of life, for our spouse and children and friends, for healing or employment or guidance, we can do so with the same attitude of heart Jesus had when He taught His disciples to pray to the Father, "Your will be done on earth as it is in heaven" (Mt. 6:10).

Jesus Himself expressed that same attitude a few hours before His death. He concluded an agonizing prayer session in Gethsemane—a time when He even asked the Father to let Him avoid the cross—with these words: "Nevertheless not My will, but Yours, be done" (Lk. 22:42). This surrender, after an intense, honest struggle, kept Him in a spirit of oneness with His Father.

We may have questions about praying, "Your will be done." Does that mean we are secretly giving up on what we just prayed for? Are we not saying that our prayer was offered without the true conviction that it was right and that God should answer it? Are we not falsely humble in trying not to bother God with our little wishes, and saying, "That's okay. I understand," if He does not grant our requests? If so, we've got it all wrong!

Helmut Thielicke wrote:

> This is just what the words "Thy will be done" do not mean. They mean, "Thou understandest my prayer better than I understand it myself (Rom. 8:26). Thou knowest most whether I need hunger or bread. Whatever may come, I will still say, 'Yes, dear Lord' (Mt. 15:27). For I know that in everything, no matter what it may be, Thy will gives me fulfillment—beyond my asking and my comprehension."

When we pray "Your will be done," we are choosing to agree with God. We are saying to Him what

Jesus said to His disciples, "My food is to do the will of Him who sent Me" (Jn. 4:34). And we are echoing the Lord's prayer in Gethsemane. Whether or not He gives us bread or a job or a mate or a child, His will done His way is best.

We will not discover the confidence of being in agreement with God, however, if we have not first been honest about the thoughts and emotions of our own hearts. Integrity of soul is basic to overcoming disappointment with God and developing confidence in prayer.

CONVERSE INSTEAD OF TALK

A common hindrance to confident praying is the feeling that no one is listening. We feel like the wife who tries to talk to her husband while he is reading the sports page of the newspaper or the father who is talking to his teenagers while they are listening to music. No feedback, no response, not even an occasional, "Uh-huh."

When this happens, we begin to see prayer as nothing more than ritual. We have lost sight of the truth that God is deeply interested in us and listening intently to every word of our prayers. Prayer is intended to be a spirited interaction between us and a loving Being with whom we have an intimate and growing relationship. "We have almost forgotten," wrote A. W. Tozer in *Pursuit Of God*, "that God is a person and, as such, can be cultivated [in a relationship] as any person can." When we feel that God is not listening, we need to focus on two vital aspects of prayer.

Confidence In Listening To God

Prayer is not merely what we say to God. It is responding thoughtfully to what He has already said and what He is constantly saying to us through His Word. For this reason, the Bible is an important part of our ongoing conversation with the Lord.

One way to develop conversation with God is to open the Scriptures to a psalm or paragraph from one of the Epistles. Read thoughtfully to discover what the text is telling you about the thoughts, affections, and values of God. Listen carefully and reverently to the mind of the One who inspired these words. Ask Him to help you discover the interests and desires of His heart. Then respond conversationally from your own heart to what you are hearing. As you do, you will begin to develop confidence that you know what is important to God. You will also begin to discover what God is doing in your own heart.

As a husband prays in response to the words of 1 Corinthians 13, for example, he will know God's mind about love and apply it to his relationship with his wife. It may be the words *love is patient* that impress him about how tersely he's been treating her. This, in turn, should lead to a welcome and much-needed change in his attitude and behavior.

"Be silent," Francois Fénelon wrote, "and listen to God. Let your heart be in such a state of preparation that His Spirit may impress upon you such virtues as will please Him. This silence of all outward and earthly affection and of human thoughts within us is essential if we are to hear this voice."

It won't be an audible voice. But you will know it's the voice of the Spirit when you hear the truths of Scripture speaking gently, lovingly, and forcefully to the circumstances and concerns of your life.

One night when my grandson Nathan was extremely ill, I awakened and prayed for him. While I remained in an attitude of prayer, silent before the Lord, I became aware of a way I had not been sensitive to the needs of my wife, Shirley. I saw how my attitudes had not been in line with the words and heart of God. I recognized a need in her life that I had been blind to for years. I asked God's forgiveness and help. The next day I began to make the appropriate change in behavior toward her. What a difference it has made! I am convinced that is how God may speak to us when we are silent before Him.

Confidence In Responding To God

Listening to God will lead to actions as well as words. Words are just the beginning. If we're reading 1 Corinthians 15, for example, we will exalt the Lord for the great victory of the resurrection and the hope that goes with it. But our response will go beyond that. It will give us greater confidence as we face a defeated spiritual enemy. It will give us words to say to the terminally ill. It will give us power as we face the everyday tumults of life. It may cause us to forsake a sinful attitude or habit.

When we pray, we must be ready to take action. The deeper the prayer goes into the Scripture, into the mind of God, the more radical the action may be. It may lead us to someone's living room to share a deep burden. It may carry us back into the past to deal with some unresolved hurt we have received or inflicted. It may drastically change our plans. We may end up in some strange place doing things we never thought possible. This is because our prayer is to God, and He is not a placid, inert Being. He is the living God, who steps into our lives with His awesome power and changes us in dramatic and unpredictable ways as we respond to Him. Or He may leave us right where we are. That's okay. He's God!

When we bow before God with our needs and our requests, we think we're the initiators. But it may be that all prayer is a response to Him. This is what Norway's Ole Hallesby taught in his classic book, *Prayer*. He saw Jesus' words "Behold, I stand at the door and knock" (Rev. 3:20) as the key that opens the door to prayer. And how does Christ knock? Through the conditions and circumstances of our experience that drive us to Him in prayer. As I think of it, my prayers for little Nathan were a response. Jesus had been knocking on the door of my life through the physical needs of my grandson.

DEFER TO GOD'S PERSPECTIVE

You've had it happen to you, I'm sure. You call the auto dealer and ask for the service department.

"Can you hold?" the cheerful voice says. In a few seconds the "elevator music" starts. Every so often a recording assures you that your call will be answered. You wait and wait, imagining that an inane conversation about last night's ball game or some television program is keeping you in limbo. After a while you're ready to hang up. It would take less time to get in the car and drive over to the place!

Sometimes it seems that God has put us on hold. He may be doing some great things in our lives, but our deepest, most cherished request is not being granted. We know He's still there, but He is simply not responding.

Hannah of the Old Testament knew what it was like to feel rejected by God (1 Sam. 1:1-18). She was one of two women married to a man named Elkanah. Peninnah, the other wife, had borne him children, but Hannah was barren in a day when childlessness was considered a sign of God's displeasure. To make matters worse, Peninnah took cruel delight in mocking Hannah's barrenness whenever the family made their annual trip to the house of God to offer a sacrifice.

Hannah's distress lasted for years even though she was a devout and faithful woman. She prayed and prayed. Yet God didn't answer. On one trip to the house of God "she was in bitterness of soul, and prayed to the Lord and wept in anguish" (v.10).

But that is not the end of Hannah's story. In God's time, and at just the right time, God gave Hannah a son. She became the mother of Samuel (vv.19-20), who in time would become a priest and prophet who would change the course of history.

In God's time, Hannah's sense of spiritual rejection was changed to joy. In an overwhelming song of praise to God, Hannah showed that her deepest longing was not for a son but to know that she was accepted and approved by God (2:1-10). In time, Hannah's bitterness was turned to joy. For every generation to come, her experience would show that what counts is not whether God immediately answers our prayers. The issue is whether we are humbly waiting on His wisdom and timing.

When Hannah's experience is combined with the rest of Scripture, we begin to see some of the many reasons for deferring not to our emotions but to the wisdom of God.

Confidence In God's Perspective

Our perspective is like looking through a pinhole. We can't see the whole picture. If we could, we would see that what we long for may not be good for us or for those we love. How many times I have been thankful that God has not given me everything I've asked Him for. How much better off I would have been if I had tempered my prayers with the awareness that it is only when we get to heaven that we will see the whole picture. Then we "shall know just as [we] also [are] known" (1 Cor. 13:12). P. T. Forsythe wrote, "We shall come one day to a heaven when we shall gratefully see that God's great refusals were sometimes the truest answers to our prayers."

Confidence In God's Wisdom

God knows our deepest need. A single mother prayed for $2,000 to bring her financial relief. God denied the request as she expressed it. Instead of giving her the money, God gave her a job that she could handle. Then He gave her a friend who helped her to learn to manage her finances. In time she was able to look back and see that God did answer her request, but in a way that reflected His wisdom. The best part is that she grew in her trust in God.

Confidence In God's Timing

The house sells later than we wanted or the baby arrives 2 weeks sooner than we expected. God's timing is always best because of His ability to orchestrate the circumstances of our lives.

Confidence In God's Goodness

We may have prayed a long time for our wife or husband to treat us with more respect, but that does not happen until God leads us to stop downgrading our spouse in public.

The answer may not come because we are refusing to forgive someone, or we are controlled by an obsession, or we are seething in such anger that our holiness is corrupted. Or we "ask amiss" so that we can indulge some base desire (Jas. 4:3). We need to do the work of examination, confession, and repentance before our prayer is answered.

Oswald Chambers understood that waiting is part of prayer. About the verse, "Men always ought to pray and not lose heart" (Lk. 18:1), he wrote:

> Jesus taught His disciples the prayer of patience. If you are right with God and God delays the answer to your prayer, don't misjudge Him. Don't think of Him as an unkind friend, or an unnatural father, or an unjust judge, but keep at it. Your prayer will certainly be answered, for "everyone who asks receives." Pray and do not cave in. Your heavenly Father will explain it all one day. He cannot just yet because He is developing your character. "Forget the character," you say. "I want Him to grant my request." And He says, "What I am doing far exceeds what you can see or know. Trust Me."

The psalmist Asaph learned to overcome such disillusionment when he was reminded of the wider perspective of God. In Psalm 73 he said:

> *Truly God is good to Israel, to such as are pure in heart. But as for me, my feet had almost stumbled; my steps had nearly slipped. For I was envious of the boastful, when I saw the prosperity of the wicked. For there are no pangs in their death, but their strength is firm. They are not in trouble as other men . . . . Surely I have cleansed my heart in vain, and washed my hands in innocence. For all day long I have been plagued, and chastened every morning . . . . When I thought how to understand this, it was too painful for me—until I went into the sanctuary of God; then I*

understood their end. Surely You set them in slippery places; You cast them down to destruction. Oh, how they are brought to desolation, as in a moment! They are utterly consumed with terrors. As a dream when one awakes, so, Lord, when You awake, You shall despise their image. Thus my heart was grieved, and I was vexed in my mind. I was so foolish and ignorant; I was like a beast before You. Nevertheless I am continually with You; You hold me by my right hand. You will guide me with Your counsel, and afterward receive me to glory. Whom have I in heaven but You? And there is none upon earth that I desire besides You. My flesh and my heart fail; but God is the strength of my heart and my portion forever (Ps. 73:1-5,13-26).

ENJOY GOD WHILE WAITING

The psalmist Asaph showed us that there is more to trusting God than deferring to His wisdom. Another way to become confident in prayer is to learn to actually enjoy Him while waiting for Him to meet our needs. Nothing we are waiting for can begin to compare with the privilege of knowing Him. Nothing else is as important to us as God Himself.

Certainly there are times when we will be overwhelmed by our troubles and crushed by our sense of disappointment and grief. Like Hannah, we will have times when we are beside ourselves with frustrated longings. Yet there will also be many other times when we can laugh for joy because of what God is doing for us.

Confidence In What We Know About Him

As we learn to wait for God, we can begin to find delight in what we already know about Him. We can accept the invitation of the psalmist to enter His gates with thanksgiving and His courts with praise, and to bless His name (Ps. 100:4).

Thank Him. God has done so much for us. If our boss or parents had done one-tenth that much for us, we would express our gratitude in lavish terms. We are to do the same with God.

O Lord my God, I will give thanks to You forever (Ps. 30:12).

Jesus gave thanks to the Father (Lk. 10:21). Paul's prayers were filled with expressions of gratitude (Eph. 5:20). We too should give joyful thanks to the Lord.

Praise Him. We praise God for who He is, and we thank Him for what He has done. The Bible is brimming with expressions of praise to the Lord.

Praise, O servants of the Lord, praise the name of the Lord! Blessed be the name of the Lord from this time forth and forevermore! From the rising of the sun to its going down the Lord's name is to be praised (Ps. 113:1-3).

Other passages of praise to the Lord include Psalm 146:1-2, Hebrews 13:15, and Revelation 4:11. Let's lift up our praise to God in prayer and express our worship and adoration in praise. "He is [our] praise" (Dt. 10:21).

Confidence In What He Has Promised

Another way to enjoy God is to rejoice in the promises He gives us about prayer. Paul named three promises in this classic prayer passage:

Be anxious for nothing, but in everything by prayer and supplication, with thanksgiving, let your requests be made known to God; and the peace of God, which surpasses all understanding, will guard your hearts and minds through Christ Jesus (Phil. 4:6-7).

The Promise Of God's Peace. The antidote to anxiety is prayer. The commitment of God is that when we roll our burdens onto His shoulders, He will give us peace. Many Christians will testify that in the dark night of fear when they brought their burden to the Lord, He gave them peace and they could sleep (Ps. 4:8). Therefore, we can rejoice to know that when we bring our concerns and burdens and cares to the Lord, He will give us peace.

The Promise Of God's Protection. Our minds and hearts will be protected when we pray. He who is our fortress guards us when the enemy attacks (Ps. 31:1-3). Therefore, we can rejoice in the protection we know He gives us.

The Promise Of God's Presence. Paul expressed it this way: "The God of peace will be with you" (Phil. 4:9). In our storm, going through the valley, or when we feel the most alone, prayer reminds us of God's presence. We can rejoice in His promise to be with us wherever we may be.

Praying Through
The Bible

The Scriptures were written by people who felt the same desires and faced the same discouragements as we do. They too were dismayed at times by their circumstances. They knew what it was like to cry out to a silent God, to come to the end of themselves, and to feel their emotions going "over the edge." Yet the people of the Bible are important to us because they lived long enough to recover their sense of joy and confidence in God.

As we struggle through our own fears and disappointments, we can find renewed hope by using their thoughts as a reflection of our own hearts and prayers. Psalm 42 is a good example. With a thirsty, downcast soul, the author cried out to the Lord and expressed the honest emotions of his heart until he rediscovered truths he had forgotten.

First we will quote a verse, then we'll show how you might pray, based on what the verse says:

"As the deer pants for the water brooks, so pants my soul for You, O God. My soul thirsts for God, for the living God. When shall I come and appear before God?" (Ps. 42:1-2).
Lord, those words express how empty I feel. I feel so dry

and tired and weak from running. My strength is gone. I don't know how much longer I can go on. If You don't help me I'm not going to make it.

I know that someday I will stand before You. But I long to hear from You now. What do You want from me? What do You want me to do?

> Yes, I will yet praise You, Lord. You are my only hope. I praise You for Your goodness. Forgive me for doubting You.

"My tears have been my food day and night, while they continually say to me, 'Where is your God?'" (v.3).
Father, I do wonder where You are and why You aren't helping me. I've been so open in the past about trusting You. But now I feel uncomfortable when I'm with people who have heard me talk about how faithful and trustworthy You are.

"I went with them to the house of God, with the voice of joy and praise" (v.4).
Things used to be so different, Lord. I used to enjoy You in the presence of Your people. We laughed and prayed together. Yet now I feel so alone. Those times of joy seem so far away.

"Why are you cast down, O my soul? And why are you disquieted within me? Hope in God, for I shall yet praise Him" (v.5).
Yes, Father, I too know better. As I listen to my own complaint, I know deep inside that You can still be trusted. I

do know that it is right to keep on trusting You. Like the psalmist, I even believe that in Your wisdom, and at the right time, You will help me. I know I will laugh again. I know the day is coming when I will praise You. O Lord, how I long for that day.

"The Lord will command His lovingkindness in the daytime, and in the night His song shall be with me— a prayer to the God of my life" (v.8).
I do believe that the day is coming when You will again let me experience Your kindness. I believe that You will once again give me songs in the night.

"I will say to God my Rock, 'Why have You forgotten me? Why do I go mourning?'" (v.9).
Father, even though I know You will help me, my fears keep coming back over me like waves. In spite of my faith in You, and even though I know You are my rock and my hiding place, I still feel so forgotten and alone. Why do You have to let me, Your child, spend my time mourning rather than praising You?

"Why are you cast down, O my soul? And why are you disquieted within me? Hope in God; for I shall yet praise Him, the help of my countenance and my God" (v.11).
Yes, I will yet praise You, Lord. You are my only hope. I praise You for Your goodness. Forgive me for doubting You. I will wait for You. I will wait for You to restore my joy!

Your Next Prayer

Your next prayer could change your life. Go back to page 72. How did you fill in the blank? Are any of the disappointments on pages 73-74 affecting you?

It's time to act. Ask God to help you push through those roadblocks, overcome those hindrances, and begin praying as you'd like to. If you get discouraged, don't let that stop you. Keep praying. You will soon pray with renewed confidence.

Or maybe you need to start with the most basic step. Perhaps you are not sure you have a personal relationship with God. You realize you are a sinner (Rom. 3:23), but you need to know this: You can't save yourself (Eph. 2:8-9). Jesus, the sinless Son of God, lived the perfect life we could never live (1 Pet. 2:22). Jesus died on the cross to pay the penalty for all our sin (1 Cor. 15:3-4). Christ's resurrection is proof that His sacrifice was acceptable to God (Rev. 1:4-6). We receive the Lord as our Savior by faith (Jn. 3:16).

Ask God to save you from the deserved penalty of your own sins. Trust Him to rescue you. This request will be the most important prayer you will ever pray. It is this prayer for salvation that provides an unshakable foundation for all of the other prayers you will offer up to God.

FOUR

How Can I Understand The Bible?

I f scholars disagree about how to interpret the Bible, how can we hope to make sense of the Scriptures? While such a question can seem overwhelming, it doesn't need to be. What *can* be understood by the average layman is far more important than what scholars disagree about.

Most important, the Author of the Bible has not left the reader alone. Paul signaled God's commitment to help us when he wrote, "Reflect on what I am saying, for the Lord will give you insight into all this" (2 Tim. 2:7 NIV). With this confidence, we offer in the following pages a simple rule that can provide focus for a lifetime of study and discovery.

MARTIN R. DE HAAN II

How To Make The Bible Say Anything

An American President once said he would rather live in Russia than in America. What President would make such a remark? It was said by the Great Emancipator himself, Abraham Lincoln.

But he's being quoted out of context. He actually said, "I shall prefer emigrating to some country where they make no pretense of loving liberty—to Russia, for instance." Lincoln wrote these words while expressing regret about a dangerous trend he saw in America. He feared that many wanted to change "all men are created equal" to "all men are created equal, except non-whites." Lincoln suggested that if that happened, he would be more comfortable in a land where the government didn't pretend to stand for liberty. The context makes all the difference.

But did you know that though Lincoln hated slavery, the Bible condones it? The Bible tells slaves to obey their masters (Eph. 6:5). It even appears to encourage us to view Africans differently than we view other people when it says, "Can the Ethiopian change his skin, or the leopard its spots?" (Jer. 13:23). Why would the Ethiopian want to change his skin unless it were a less than desirable condition, and why would the author link Ethiopians to leopards unless he wanted his readers to think of black people in less than human terms?

Again, these words have been twisted out of their original setting and intent. Quoted in context, Jeremiah was *not* putting dark skin in an unfavorable light, anymore than he was being critical of the beauty and distinctive design of a leopard's coat. Jeremiah's message is that *if* the leopard could change his own spots, and *if* an Ethiopian could change the color of his skin, *then* "may you also do good who are accustomed to do evil" (Jer. 13:23). The immediate context shows that Jeremiah was saying we cannot change our own hearts any more than we can change the color of our skin. Any changes *we* make are merely cosmetic. The context shows exactly what Jeremiah meant to say.

But did Paul encourage slaves to obey their masters? Yes, and his comments must be understood in light of the times and spirit in which the apostle wrote. Slavery in Roman days was often the result of war or unpaid debts. Paul taught Christians to be free if they could (1 Cor. 7:21). If that was not possible, he encouraged them to show by their behavior that their well-being was not in the hands of human masters but in the hands of God, even in bad circumstances (1 Cor. 7:20-24). When two Christians found themselves in a master-slave relationship, Paul appealed to them to treat each other as equals and as brothers (Eph. 6:5-9; Phile. 15-16).

Context. If the immediate and wider contexts are not considered, a person can make the Bible say anything he wants it to say.

One Rule That Helps You Study The Bible With Confidence

One basic rule of Bible study underlies all others. It is the law of context. In what setting and with what intent were the words written? Equipped with this one basic principle, a student can begin immediately to spend a lifetime looking for and discovering the treasures of the Bible. Let's begin by seeing how this pursuit of context will lead naturally into a careful consideration of (1) immediate setting, (2) normal usage of words, (3) the Bible as a whole, and (4) foundational truths of sound doctrine.

CONTEXT OF IMMEDIATE SETTING

Even experienced Bible students are often surprised to see what a familiar Bible quotation means when understood in light of its immediate setting. Difficult problems of understanding often evaporate simply by determining how a text is framed by the main idea running through that section of Scripture.

Behind every statement of Scripture is an immediate setting. This provides clues as to what was on the author's mind. In every immediate setting there are similar or recurring ideas and words that help to signal the main idea. Once that main idea is identified, it becomes the key to opening up the meaning of the text in question.

To discover the flow of ideas streaming through a passage, good Bible students become childlike and at the same time scientific in asking questions: Who is the author? To whom is he writing? Why? When? Where? How? Wherefore?

> Ripped from context, noble words can be filled with an evil spirit.

Careful students interrogate the page to expose its logic and flow of ideas. They don't assume that the author is saying what they think he is saying, until they have done their spade work. They don't try to plant an idea in "unworked ground." They dig and turn over the soil of the biblical environment until they discover the growing, living, life-changing ideas that *God* has planted.

Let's look at some examples of specific texts whose immediate contexts have been ignored.

Misquote 1:
"The Bible says that if you confess your sins you'll be saved."

It really says, "If we confess our sins, He is faithful and just to forgive us our sins" (1 Jn. 1:9). These familiar words are often quoted as a formula for salvation. But the presence of the word *we* in the immediate context makes it clear that John was not addressing the unsaved. Rather, he was talking to people who were already believers in Christ (vv.6,7,8,10), and he was showing them how to be restored to a right family relationship with the God who had saved them. If we don't consider the immediate context, we might conclude that we are saved by admitting our sins rather than by believing the gospel of Christ.

Misquote 2:
"The Bible says that it's wrong to wear jewelry."

The actual quote is: "Do not let your adornment be merely outward—arranging the hair, wearing gold, or putting on fine apparel" (1 Pet. 3:3). Some have used these words to say that godly women should not style their hair, use cosmetics, or wear jewelry. But if we read on, we find the words, "rather let it be the hidden person of the heart" (v.4). By these additional words we see that the apostle's main purpose was not to tell women that they either should or should not style their hair or wear jewelry. He was saying that they should focus on the beauty of a gentle and quiet spirit rather than relying on outward appearance.

To focus on whether or not jewelry or cosmetics are permissible can cause us to miss issues of the heart that Peter was concerned about.

Misquote 3:
"The Bible says that studying for knowledge isn't necessary."

It actually says, "If any of you lacks wisdom, let him

ask of God, who gives to all liberally and without reproach, and it will be given to him" (Jas. 1:5). These words have been seen by some as a promise that we can receive unlearned skills and knowledge if we just pray. More than a few college students have claimed this promise before taking an exam they had not prepared for.

The immediate context, however, is describing a reason for the joy we can have when difficult circumstances test our faith. James' promise is not that we can be successful without effort, but rather that God does not leave us alone when He allows trouble or temptation to come into our lives. James assured us that if we don't know how to let God do His work in us, we can have wisdom for the asking.

Later in the same letter, James told his readers how to recognize this wisdom when it comes. He said it is not marked by envy or selfish ambition, but is "pure, then peaceable, gentle, willing to yield, full of mercy and good fruits, without partiality and without hypocrisy" (Jas. 3:17). This is the kind of wisdom James had in mind.

Misquote 4:
"The Bible says that I can do anything with God's strength."

More specifically it says, "I can do all things through Christ who strengthens me" (Phil. 4:13). This optimistic comment is often taken to mean that if our faith is strong enough we can do anything we set our mind to do. But the immediate setting in which Paul said this is important. The apostle was talking specifically about his ability to live by God's strength in times of great poverty as well as in times of plenty. Paul wanted us to know that the person whose confidence is in the strength God supplies can live and thrive in all kinds of situations.

Misinterpretations of Bible texts can often be avoided if the immediate setting is taken into account.

These are just a few examples to show that misinterpretations of Bible texts can often be avoided if the immediate setting is taken into account. Looking at the verses that precede and follow a passage is a natural and logical first step in understanding the Bible. It is a way of giving God the same consideration we want for ourselves. No one wants to be quoted out of context.

CONTEXT OF PLAIN AND NORMAL MEANING

The second rule of context says that the language of the Bible can be taken at face value. The Word of God does not have to be decoded to find deeper, hidden meanings. When studied and interpreted in context, the authors of Scripture say what they mean and mean what they say.

Take for instance the account of Balaam and the talking donkey recorded in Numbers 22. According to this familiar account, the donkey on which a disobedient prophet was riding became frightened when she saw an angel with a drawn sword. The donkey lurched sideways, crushed the foot of her owner against a rock, refused to go any farther, and complained to her rider in complete sentences.

Because donkeys don't talk, some might say this is simply a parable meant to show that even dumb animals sometimes make more sense than their human owners. Others, however, could claim deeper truths.

For example, someone might point out that the story of Balaam and the donkey is actually a visualization of what happens when we find ourselves faced with the pains of self-conflict. To illustrate this internal struggle, the crushed foot represents the physical pain we often incur in the process of acting against our own conscience. The talking donkey depicts how our own stubborn thoughts can turn around and talk back to us. Then there's the angel. That's our human spirit. At the right moment, it intervenes with our plans, startles our troubled mind, and talks to us from a different level of consciousness.

The trouble with the above interpretation is that it says far more about the imagination of the interpreter than about the text. More seriously, such imagination, as spiritual as it may sound, actually twists, ignores, and denies the real meaning of the Word of God. Emptying words of their plain meaning and filling them with spiritual content doesn't honor the words nor the Author of the Bible.

The story of Balaam and the donkey isn't treated by the text as a parable. Neither is it about personal internal conflict, even though that is in the text. The plain, normal language of the text calls for us to interpret it as a real historical narrative. It presents a record of real events that show God's miraculous ability not only to deal with a rebel prophet but, more important, to miraculously bless and preserve His chosen people Israel as well.

The normal meaning of figures of speech

We use word pictures in everyday conversation—not to hide our ideas but to express them. Take for example the expression, "I'm getting cold feet." Context and normal usage make its meaning obvious. If a person were to make this statement while ice fishing, and just before saying, "I wish I'd worn that other pair of socks," it would have a literal meaning. But if someone were to say these words a couple of days before signing papers for a home mortgage, we could probably assume that something else was in view, especially if the person then said, "I'm going to refigure our budget."

Christ often used figures of speech with plain and obvious meaning. On one occasion He said to the apostle Peter, "I will give you the keys of the kingdom of heaven, and whatever you bind on earth will be bound in heaven, and whatever you loose on earth will be loosed in heaven" (Mt. 16:19). No one needs to question whether Jesus was talking about real physical keys or keys as a figure of speech. The kingdom of heaven is not enclosed within a material wall with a door that requires an actual key. Neither was Christ promising, as some have imagined, that Peter and the disciples would be able to bind anything they wanted to bind (including Satan).

In time, the "keys" would have a specific meaning for Peter. In Matthew 16, Christ gave Peter authority to open the doors of Christendom. He used that authority for Jews on the Day of Pentecost (Acts 2), for Samaritans when he laid hands on the people who believed the message of Philip (Acts 8), and for Gentiles when he preached in the house of Cornelius (Acts 10). Peter had opened the door to all nations to receive Jesus as Savior and King. No one would ever again be able to "bind" a Jew or a Gentile who believes in Christ from coming into the kingdom of God.

When read in context, there is usually a plain and ordinary sense to figurative and symbolic language. In many cases, the Bible even immediately explains its own symbolism. But what if the intent of the author is not clear? What if it's not clear whether the Bible is using words in a plain or figurative sense? Then the safest rule is to go with the literal meaning of the text in its immediate context. Because of the integrity of Scripture, we can be confident that the ultimate truth in view will correspond to the plain and ordinary sense of the words. "Good fruit" won't mean "bad results."

CONTEXT OF THE BIBLE AS A WHOLE

A third rule of contextual interpretation is to consider the passage in its relation to the whole

Bible. Because the 39 books of the Old Testament and the 27 books of the New Testament are all "chapters" of one Book, those who want to live by the whole counsel of God need increasingly to be able to see each individual part in light of the whole.

The many perspectives of the whole Bible cannot be quickly mastered. Gathering and combining the insights of the whole Bible is the process of a lifetime. This is one reason the Bible says that God gives pastors and teachers to His people. Those who know more than we do about the Bible can help us to balance our understanding of individual passages with complementing perspectives.

The Lord Himself showed how important it is to be able to see one passage in light of another. On the occasion of His temptation in the wilderness, He skillfully quoted from the Old Testament to offset the devil's own use of Scripture. The devil first challenged the Lord to prove that He was the Son of God by turning stones into bread. Jesus refused, and quoted Deuteronomy 8:3 to make it clear that He was determined to live by His Father's provisions rather than His own. Satan then transported Jesus to the highest point of the temple and again challenged Him to prove that He was the Son of God. Satan quoted from a messianic section of Psalm 91, which says, "He shall give His angels charge over you," and "In their hands they shall bear you up, lest you dash your foot against a stone" (vv. 11-12; Mt. 4:6). But Jesus replied by saying, "It is also written: 'Do not put the Lord your God to the test'" (Mt. 4:7 NIV). By quoting Moses, Jesus indicated that it was not right for a man to willfully put God to the test. Something Moses wrote as many as 1,500 years earlier allowed Jesus to show that it is not our right to arrange circumstances in such a way as to attempt to force God's hand of provision.

Let's look at a few examples that show why the context of the whole Bible is so important.

Example 1:
What is "also written" about forgiveness?

While individual sections of the Bible might lead you to conclude that it is never right to withhold forgiveness, the counsel of the whole Bible is that there is a time to forgive and a time not to forgive.

There is a time to forgive. Paul wrote that we are to forgive others as God has forgiven us (Eph. 4:32). Jesus said that if we don't forgive others, God will withhold forgiveness from us (Mt. 6:14-15). And from the cross, Jesus freely forgave those who applauded His death when He said, "Father, forgive them, for they do not know what they do" (Lk. 23:34). If you read only these passages, you might conclude that Christlike people will always and immediately forgive any harm done to them. But these passages represent only part of the picture.

There is a time not to forgive. "It is also written" that God forgives us in response to our repentance (Lk. 18:9-14). In the process of extending "family forgiveness," which renews and restores children of God who have sinned, God forgives *when* we confess our sins (1

Jn. 1:9). Forgiveness is not unconditional. It depends on the willingness of sinners to acknowledge and believe what God says about their sin. Many passages of Scripture show that we should not freely forgive those who have knowingly sinned against us but have not shown any remorse (Mt. 18:15-18; 1 Cor. 5:7-13).

But what about Jesus' words from the cross, "Father, forgive them"? Didn't He freely forgive those who had carried out His execution? Yes, but the key to understanding His words is found in the immediate context. He went on to say, "Father, forgive them, for they do not know what they do." This was not a request for their salvation, but rather a plea for individuals who didn't know that their hands had lifted the Creator of the universe onto an executioner's cross. Jesus mercifully asked that they not be held accountable for being chosen by time and circumstance to be the hands of the whole fallen human race.

The key to forgiveness is found in the following questions: What do love and truth require? What would Jesus do in this situation? (For more help on this subject, see the RBC booklet *When Forgiveness Seems Impossible* CB941.)

Example 2:
What is "also written" about our spiritual enemy?
While some sections of the Bible seem to leave the impression that Satan is no longer a threat to us, other parts of Scripture show us that in some ways we have power over him, and in some ways we don't.

We have power over the devil. Some passages of

Scripture picture Satan as a defeated enemy. The apostle James made it clear that those who are in Christ can resist the efforts of the devil and by so doing cause him to flee from them. James said, "Submit to God. Resist the devil and he will flee from you" (Jas. 4:7). The apostle John told the Lord's children that the One who is in them is greater than their spiritual enemy (1 Jn. 4:4). Jesus also displayed the advantage of His family when He sent out His disciples to cast out demons and to heal all kinds of sickness (Mt. 10:1).

We don't have power over the devil. It is "also written" that while we have power to resist Satan, we don't have authority over him. God has not yet "bound the dragon" (Rev. 20:2), who is still prowling like a roaring lion (1 Pet. 5:8). Neither has God given us authority to bind the enemy ourselves. Instead, the Scriptures encourage us to have a healthy respect for the one who still troubles the world. The New Testament writer Jude reminded us that even Michael the archangel did not presume to act as if he had authority over Satan, but instead said, "The Lord rebuke you!" (Jude 9). And while Jesus had at one point sent His apostles to cast out demons and heal all kinds of sicknesses (Mt. 10:1), He showed on a later occasion that the terms of their assignment and authority were subject to change (Lk. 22:35-38).

Example 3:
What is "also written" about real Christians?

While individual passages of the Bible might lead us to believe that real Christians will always prove by their actions that their faith is genuine, the whole counsel of God shows that real Christians often live far below their potential in Christ.

Real Christians will act in a Christlike way. Many sections of the Bible give us reason to expect new and consistent behavior from genuine Christians. James said simply, "Faith without works is dead" (Jas. 2:20). Paul said that anyone who is in Christ is a "new creation." He said that old things were passed away and that all things were new (2 Cor. 5:17). The apostle John agreed that true children of God have a new nature that does not express itself in a sinful life (1 Jn. 3:4-9). Throughout the whole of Scripture there is a consistent theme that God expects His children to live in a manner that shows their relation to Him.

Real Christians will disappoint us. It is "also written" that real Christians can behave in ways that are demonic (Jas. 3:13-16). The same James who wrote that "faith without works is dead" also described the dark side that remains in true Christians. He warned about the dangers of prejudice (2:1-7) and careless conversation (3:1-12), and he warned the people of God about the desires that cause believers not only to harm one another (4:1-4) but also to act like enemies of God. In a similar way, the apostle Paul acknowledged that most Christians are still preoccupied with their own interests rather than with the interests of God (Phil. 2:21). Paul confronted so much out-of-character behavior among those who claimed to be believers that he took comfort in this truth: "'The Lord knows those who are His,' and, 'Let everyone who names the name of Christ depart from iniquity'" (2 Tim. 2:19).

Reading one passage in the Bible by itself can be like looking at a piece of a jigsaw puzzle. As you analyze it, you see elements of form and color, but you understand that it is only one essential part of the bigger picture.

But there is another basic and essential element of context. There are some truths in the Bible so basic that new believers need to be quickly oriented to them. Without a grasp of these foundational truths, the Bible can be especially difficult to understand.

CONTEXT OF FOUNDATIONAL TRUTHS

This fourth rule of context, like the third, calls for a wide view of Scripture. There are some basic, foundational truths in Scripture that when understood can help to provide orientation, background, and backdrop for the interpretation of many individual passages. These truths can be discovered by self-study. But the sooner they are understood, the sooner a child of God can begin to see where individual ideas fit in the whole picture of what God has revealed.

Law And Grace

In one sense "the law of God" refers to the commandments of Moses. In a broader sense, however, law is any statement that describes the high standards of

God. Some of these laws are social. Some are moral. Some are spiritual regulations for worship.

If anyone could keep all of God's laws, that person could be assured of heaven and of continuous Christ-like spirituality. But in reality, no one has ever qualified for eternal life by keeping the law. Neither has anyone ever grown to spiritual maturity by trying to keep the commandments of God (Gal. 3:1-5). Both salvation and spirituality occur not by trying to keep the perfect principles of God but by *believing* what God has said.

The grace of God, which is offered to those who believe, is a system of mercy and undeserved help. Without grace, no one has ever been saved. Without grace, no one has ever taken the smallest step toward God. Without grace, no child of God has ever grown in Christlikeness. Grace is God's offer of relationship and help. It is His way of living His life through all who will humble themselves enough to call out and surrender to Him.

Justification And Sanctification

Justification is the legal act by which God declares righteous all who trust His Son for salvation. The only thing we can do to qualify for this status is to believe in Christ. To be justified is a free act of God's grace. We cannot earn it (Rom. 3:24).

Because of His life, death, and resurrection on our behalf, Christ our Savior can justify every wicked and ungodly person who comes to Him for grace (Rom. 4:5).

Sanctification is the process by which God continues to set apart and distinguish those who have believed in His Son. A first act of saving sanctification "sets apart" a believer for God forever. That act is followed by a planned, progressive process of being set apart from sin to God.

If the ideas of justification and sanctification are confused, we might make the mistake of thinking that our salvation has never been secured. Some who lean toward a law rather than a grace view of God will never have the assurance of sins forgiven and of full acceptance and adoption into the family of heaven. A right view of the distinction between justification and sanctification allows us to see that a believer in Christ is born into the family of God, fully justified, and ready for the lifelong process of practical sanctification.

Israel And The Church

Much confusion can be avoided by seeing the clear distinction between Israel and the church. While both worship the same God, there is a fundamental distinction.

Israel is a nation of individuals who can trace their ethnic, blood relationship back to Abraham through Isaac and Jacob. Israel gave us the Law of Moses, the Prophets, and the Messiah of the world. Israel is a nation with whom God made specific covenants for time and eternity. It is the nation that was set aside shortly after Jesus' appearance and rejection as Messiah. It is the nation, of all the nations on earth, that has been chosen by God to show Himself to the whole world. Israel is the nation, according to the Scriptures, that will be in the center of world events in the last days.

The church has no single ethnic identification. It is made up of men and women of every nation who confess Christ as Savior and Lord. Beginning at Pentecost, the church will remain on earth until supernaturally removed in an event often called "the rapture" (1 Th. 4:14-17; Jn. 14:1-3).

Four Essentials For Finding Truth In Context

While interpreting the Bible according to the rule of context, there are some timeless considerations that need to be kept in mind.

Dependence On God

The author of Psalm 119 reminded us of the role God can have in our Bible study. He prayed, "Open my eyes, that I may see wondrous things from Your law" (v.18). His confidence in God's ability to help is similar to what the apostle Paul expressed when he wrote, "Reflect on what I am saying, for the Lord will give you insight into all this" (2 Tim. 2:7 NIV).

A Good Conscience

A bad conscience creates a conflict of interest for the Bible student. Those with unconfessed sin, and therefore something to hide, are predisposed to avoid the truth. They are out of step with God, who has promised understanding to those who, by obedience, keep a good conscience (Mt. 5:8; Jn. 14:21).

Self-Study

Christians of the New Testament community of Berea are an example for all of us. They searched the

Scriptures to make sure that what the apostle Paul was telling them was true (Acts 17:11). Without personal involvement, the Scriptures remain second-hand, pre-digested, and subject to the accuracy of the teacher.

Use Of Gifted Teachers

Teachers are a gift from God (Eph. 4:11). Along with self-study, they can provide a depth and breadth of contextual knowledge. They provide orientation for new believers and reminders to those who are mature (2 Pet. 1:12-13).

The Inductive Study
Method You Can Do

While God's plan has been to give His people pastors and teachers, there is no substitute for personal study of the Scriptures. Many have found that they get more from their teachers when they become personally involved in regular and systematic Bible study.

One method of personal Bible study is called the inductive method. This method challenges the student to form conclusions only after observing and analyzing the elements of immediate context and normal word meanings. After asking the Author of Scripture for insight, the inductive student explores the inspired page with pencil in hand and the curiosity of a prospector looking for something more precious than gold (Prov. 3:13-18).

The overall strategy of the inductive student is (1) observation, (2) interpretation, and (3) application—in that order.

STEP 1: OBSERVATION
WHAT DOES THE CONTEXT SAY?

The primary purpose of this stage is to collect as many facts as possible about the context. Inductive students are curious. They don't take anything for granted. They ask and list as many questions as possible: Who? What? Why? Where? When? How? Wherefore? What words need to be looked up to determine a range of possible meanings? What logic indicators can be found and marked in words such as *therefore, then, and, also, but, however,* or *nevertheless*? What is the main point of the section? What recurring words indicate a main idea? What elements, arguments, or illustrations does the author use to support the main point?

At this stage, a chapter might be outlined or a sentence diagrammed to see how the ideas of the author relate to one another. The purpose of this stage is to discover the context.

STEP 2: INTERPRETATION
WHAT DOES THE TEXT MEAN?

Only after doing the spade work of careful observation should the inductive student ask, "What, then, does the author mean by these words as they relate to the words that precede and follow?" Not "What do these words mean to me?" But "What did they mean when they flowed from the pen of the original author? What was his intent?" While we can assume that he said what he meant and meant what he said, the only way to discover what he really meant is by observing the context.

While word forms, definitions, and a range of possible meanings may have been noted in the step of observation, it is at the point of interpreting in context that a word is best understood in the way the author was using it. Now the Scriptures come alive with the pulse and throb of the author's own heart and intent.

STEP 3: APPLICATION
WHAT DOES THIS TEXT MEAN
TO MY LIFE?

Only after discovering the meaning of a text in its own biblical time and place is the student encouraged to ask, "What does this mean to me?" Care is given to distinguish between cultural facts and timeless principles. Focus is put on the main idea. What are the primary issues of the heart? What does this say about my relationship to God? The Bible can now explode in significance.

Guidelines For
Interpreting Prophecy

To understand prophetic portions of Scripture, a Christian must be aware of one basic principle and follow six rules of interpretation.

THE PRINCIPLE OF PROPHETIC PERSPECTIVE

The prophets often described future events in one picture without indicating that they would be separated by periods of time. This has been compared to seeing mountain peaks in one view without seeing the valleys between them.

Jesus used the principle of prophetic perspective when He read the Scriptures in a Nazareth synagogue. He opened the scroll to Isaiah and read:

The Spirit of the Lord is upon Me, because He has anointed Me to preach the gospel to the poor; He has sent Me to heal the brokenhearted, to proclaim liberty to the captives and recovery of sight to the blind, to set at liberty those who are oppressed; to proclaim the acceptable year of the Lord (Lk. 4:18-19).

Then Jesus rolled up the scroll. People familiar with Isaiah 61:1-2 must have wondered why Jesus stopped in the middle of the second verse. He did not read on because the last part of verse 2, "And the day of vengeance of our God; to comfort all who mourn," speaks of the great tribulation. Jesus said He fulfilled the first part of Isaiah's prophecy (Lk. 4:21). The last part is about His second coming. The prophet, seeing it all in one look, did not know that at least 2,000 years would separate those two phases of his prophecy.

The prophecy of Joel 2:28-32 also has a double fulfillment. The first part came to pass at Pentecost, as indicated by Peter in his sermon (Acts 2:17-21). But the second part, referring to the moon turning to blood and other supernatural signs, will be fulfilled in the tribulation.

SIX RULES FOR INTERPRETING PROPHECY

1. Interpret in context
As with all Bible passages, consider the speaker, the situation, the people addressed, and the subject of the prophecy.

2. Interpret literally
Give words their normal meaning, recognizing figures of speech. When prophets specify numbers of days or years, take them literally.

3. Be careful with symbols
Don't give a prophetic passage a symbolic or spiritual meaning when literal interpretation makes

sense. For example, the earthquake of Revelation 6:12-17 is exactly that; it does not represent the breakup of society.

4. Look for immediate fulfillment

Look first for the elements of a prophecy that were fulfilled within a few years, then consider fulfillments during Christ's first and second comings.

5. Be consistent

Don't treat Christ's predictions in a different way from Old Testament prophecies.

6. Don't go too far

Some questions about endtime events must remain unanswered.

The Bible Student's One-Shelf Library

A Study Bible provides introductions and outlines for each book of the Bible, footnotes, maps, cross-references, doctrinal summaries, historical and cultural background, time charts, and a basic commentary on the text.

An Exhaustive Concordance offers an alphabetical listing of every word of the Bible and every place where that word is found. Make sure you choose a concordance that matches the translation of the Bible you use. The standard concordance for the King James Version, *Strong's Exhaustive Concordance*, has a helpful numbering system that provides a number connecting words to their root words in the original languages.

A Bible Handbook gives detailed information about the individual books of the Bible, such as the background of the author of a book, the book's purpose and destination, and the important ideas that the book presents. A Bible handbook also provides historical and cultural information pertinent to the book, appropriate maps, and a detailed outline of its message and themes.

A Bible Dictionary provides definitions and general background information for the people, places, things, and ideas of the Bible.

A One- Or Two-Volume Commentary offers helpful explanations that can show the student how others have interpreted a passage of Scripture.

Computer Bible-Study Software is by far the most revolutionary recent breakthrough in Bible study. The whole Bible can be searched instantly for words or phrases. Word studies, cross-references, topical studies, original language works, and commentaries are all built into easy-to-use study software programs that are available in both Macintosh and PC platforms.

Comprehensive Bible-study programs include several Bible translations, commentaries, language and reference tools, and other study aids—sometimes focusing on the writings of particular Bible teachers or pastors. Examples of Bible-study programs include *Online Bible* for Macintosh, and *PC Study Bible*, *Quick-Verse*, and *Logos Bible Study Library* for PC. The *Expositor's Bible Commentary* (12 volumes in book form) is available on a single CD in either platform.

Entire libraries with hundreds of books are also available in electronic form. *Ages Software*, for example, offers collections of classic Christian works and the writings of Spurgeon, Luther, and other Reformation leaders.

Bible software has come a long way in the last 10 years. This technology enables Bible students to be good stewards of their time and money. Imagine being able to purchase hundreds of books on a single CD and then using the power of a computer to quickly search through and access the information you need. These computer programs have become a wonderful asset to pastors, Sunday school teachers, and Bible students of every level of spiritual growth.

Online Study Helps. One example of many sites on the Internet that provide Bible-study helps is www.biblestudytools.net.

How To Use A Commentary

———

Commentaries are books that analyze and explain the text of the Bible. The better ones deal with every verse—giving the meaning of the words, explaining the setting, and offering light from other places in the Bible. Many of them are the product of careful, prayerful, and diligent scholarship. Some are published in one or two volumes, others in entire sets. Commentaries are indispensable to effective Bible study, but they must be used properly. We recommend that you consult them only after you have carefully worked through the passage yourself.

After you have done your best to understand a passage, consult three or four good commentaries. If you use them before you have done your own work, you will short-circuit your thinking. If you evaluate only what others have written, you are robbing yourself of the thrill of discovery and the joy of creative, Spirit-led Bible study.

What will the effective use of good commentaries do for you as you study the Bible? Following is a list of some of the things using commentaries could do for you as you pursue a deeper understanding of God's Word.

1. Confirm your understanding of a passage.

When you find that all of the commentaries you consult interpret the passage essentially the way you did, you can be confident that you are on target in your conclusions.

2. Refine your understanding of a passage.

The commentators may present insights that didn't come to your mind, thus deepening and enriching your understanding of the passage.

3. Lead you to reevaluate your interpretations.

Occasionally you will find that the commentaries present conclusions somewhat different from your interpretation. You may also discover that the commentators differ from one another. When this happens, you'll be glad you did your own spade work. It will help you evaluate the views expressed. After careful thought, you may select an interpretation quite different from the one you had when you started.

4. Show you that your understanding of the passage was almost entirely wrong.

Reading the commentaries may give you information that will make you realize you have overlooked or misunderstood an important element in the passage or verse you have been studying. When this happens, go back to the text and think it through again.

"The Bible Is Ours"

Many people feel they won't be able to understand the Bible, no matter how hard they try. Bill and Gwen Petroski felt that way—till something happened that opened God's way for them.

Here's their story: "One of the greatest blessings in our lives has been the discovery that we can read and understand the Bible for ourselves. You see, both of us were raised in a religion that did not emphasize the Bible.

"After we were married, we began a spiritual quest. We felt vaguely dissatisfied. We wanted our children to know God and to have Christian values. So we began to search.

"Then the day came when both of us received Jesus Christ as personal Savior. We began attending a Bible-preaching church and hearing the Word of God proclaimed. Gradually we realized that the Bible is ours and that we can read and study it for ourselves."

Gwen: "I remember vividly the first time I read the book of Hebrews. One Sunday morning I read it through in one sitting. Tears flowed then and still do now as I realize that all barriers between God and me are broken down, and that I have access to God."

Bill: "When I first read Ephesians 2:8-9 and understood salvation by grace through faith alone,

I was filled with gratitude to God. This passage will always be one of my favorites.

"We now know that the Bible is ours. As we continue to read and study it, it means more to us than ever before. We are trying to put its teachings into practice so that our four girls will see that it can be real to them."

These testimonies of Bill and Gwen highlight the thrill of discovering rich spiritual truth through personal Bible study. The Holy Spirit ministers to believers in a special way through the Word, but He also brings understanding to non-Christians who read it with a sincere desire to know God.

Carl Armerding told about an Australian sheepherder and his wife who came to know Christ this way. They began reading the book of Romans out of the old family Bible just to while away the evening hours. After some time, the man said, "Wife, if this book is right, we are guilty sinners before God. We are condemned." At the conclusion of their reading a few days later, he exclaimed, "Wife, if this book is right, we need not remain condemned. A man called Jesus Christ took our punishment by dying for us. He's alive again, and He wants us to believe on Him."

Although these people had very little education, they were able to gather from the Scriptures the basic truths necessary for salvation. When they began reading the Bible, they found that it was for them.

The Bible is for you—it's for everyone.

Bible-Study Checklist

Here are some questions to ask yourself when studying the Bible:

- Have I asked God for insight into His Word?
- Am I studying for relationship with Him?
- Have I read the verses immediately preceding and following the passage?
- Have I scanned the surrounding chapters?
- Have I looked up words I don't understand?
- Have I asked the questions who, what, where, when, why, how, wherefore?
- Have I looked for transitions: then, therefore, but?
- Have I identified any Old Testament quotes and checked their context?
- Have I used a Bible dictionary?
- Have I used a study Bible for parallel passages?
- Have I checked cross-references in a study Bible to see what else the Bible says about this subject?
- Have I kept from focusing on details to the exclusion of main ideas?
- Have I double-checked my interpretation with reliable commentaries?
- Have I asked what this passage tells me about God, myself, and others?
- Are there any sins to be avoided?
- Are there commands to be obeyed?
- Have I thanked God for the privilege of studying His Word?